S0-BVP-575

AUGUSTANA UNIVERSITY COLLEGE
LIBRARY

AN INTRODUCTION TO DISTRIBUTED AND PARALLEL COMPUTING

Dedicated to
my wife Valerie,
my children Vaughn, Brook, Jamie and Amanda,
my father Cecil,
and to the memory of my dear mother Elmyra

AN INTRODUCTION TO DISTRIBUTED AND PARALLEL COMPUTING

Joel M. Crichlow

The University of the West Indies

PRENTICE HALL

New York   London   Toronto   Sydney   Tokyo

First published 1988 by
Prentice Hall International (UK) Ltd,
66 Wood Lane End, Hemel Hempstead,
Hertfordshire, HP2 4RG
A division of
Simon & Schuster International Group

© 1988 Prentice Hall International (UK) Ltd

All rights reserved. No part of this publication may be
reproduced, stored in a retrieval system, or transmitted,
in any form or by any means, electronic, mechanical,
photocopying, recording or otherwise, without the
prior permission, in writing, from the publisher.
For permission within the United States of America
contact Prentice Hall Inc., Englewood Cliffs, NJ 07632.

Printed and bound in Great Britain by
A. Wheaton and Co. Ltd, Exeter

Library of Congress Cataloging-in-Publication Data

Crichlow, Joel M., 1948–
  An introduction to distributed and
  parallel computing / Joel M. Crichlow.
    p.   cm.
  Bibliography: p.
  Includes index.
  ISBN 0-13-481094-5 (pbk.)
  1. Electronic data processing – Distributed processing.
  2. Parallel processing (Electronic computers) I. Title.
QA76.9.D5C75 1987
ISBN 0-13-481086-4   68644

British Library Cataloguing in Publication Data

Crichlow, Joel M.
  An Introduction to Distributed and Parallel Computing
  1. Parallel processing (Electronic computers)
  2. Electronic data processing – Distributed processing
  I. Title
004'.35   QA76.6

ISBN 0-13-481086-4
ISBN 0-13-481094-5 pbk   68644

1 2 3 4 5 92 91 90 89 88

ISBN 0-13-481086-4
ISBN 0-13-481094-5 PBK

CONTENTS

v

AUGUSTANA UNIVERSITY COLLEGE
LIBRARY

7   PARALLEL PROGRAMMING LANGUAGES   166

PREFACE

This text introduces the reader to several different streams of activity that fall under the heading 'distributed and parallel computing'. Both hardware and software aspects are touched on. The material presented should be adequate for a university introductory level course in this subject.

The student is assumed to have had an introduction to programming, data structures, file design and operating systems. Some knowledge of computer organization would be helpful but no previous exposure to communications technology is required. Readers who do not have this background should still be able to appreciate some of the concepts that are discussed. Many of the technical terms are explained and are set in *bold italic* on their first appearance. There is a relatively extensive glossary to which one may refer in order to clarify the passages in which these terms are used subsequently.

There are seven chapters. Chapter One is an introduction to all the areas that are discussed in the following six chapters. Chapter Two presents the ways in which computer systems have been organized to facilitate distributed and parallel computing. Chapter Three gives an introduction to communications technology and computer networks. Chapter Four discusses aspects of operating systems design for distributed and parallel computing. Chapter Five deals with the popular client-server model of distributed computing. Chapter Six focuses on distributed database systems and Chapter Seven provides an informal introduction to some parallel programming languages.

There are questions at the end of each chapter to aid the reader in the assimilation of the concepts presented. For those who would like to explore any of these areas in greater detail there is a list of references following each chapter.

I must acknowledge the help of a number of people who have contributed in different ways to making this book possible. I am appreciative of the support of my colleagues at the University of the West Indies in

Computer science, Ken Cazabon, Noel Kalicharan, Krishna Brijpaul, Sheik Yussuff, Margaret Bernard, Graham Taylor, Roger Barnes and Wayne Sheppard; the entire staff in Mathematics, but, in particular, David Beckles, David Owen, Hydar Ali, Ed Farrel and Philbert Morris; and in Seismology, John Shepherd and William Aspinal.

Thanks to Professor Bruce Bolt of the University of California, Berkeley for introducing me to large scale seismic computations. I am also grateful to Professor Peter Brown, Professor Brian Spratt and others at the Computing Laboratory, University of Kent at Canterbury who contributed to making my stay there as a Research Fellow a productive one; and the editorial staff at Prentice Hall International for their guidance during the preparation of this text.

Permission was kindly granted by the following:

Addison-Wesley to take an abstract from Needham, R.M. and Herbert, A.J., 1982, *The Cambridge Distributed Computing System*, Addison-Wesley, London.

Dr R.P.A. Collinson to abstract from his paper 'Operating System Interfaces to LANs' presented at the University of Kent at Canterbury in September, 1984.

Mr Ian Utting to take an abstract from his paper 'Distributed High Quality Printer Servers' presented at the University of Kent at Canterbury in September, 1984.

John Wiley & Sons, Ltd to take an abstract from Turner, D.A., 'A new implementation technique for applicative languages', *Software – Practice and Experience*, **9**, 1979, 31–49, © 1979, John Wiley & Sons, Ltd.

John Wiley & Sons, Ltd to take an abstract from Brownbridge, D.R., Marshall, L.F. and Randell, B., 1982, 'The Newcastle Connection or UNIXes of the World Unite!', *Software – Practice and Experience*, **12**, 12, 1147–1162 © 1982, John Wiley & Sons, Ltd.

The following are trademarks: Ada (US Government, Ada Joint Program Office); Connection Machine (Thinking Machines Corporation); Cray (Cray Research, Inc.); DEC (Digital Equipment Corporation); DECnet (Digital Equipment Corporation); UNIX (AT & T Bell Laboratories).

I am indebted to my wife Valerie, my father and the other members of my family who provided all the encouragement; and thanks to God in whom 'we live, and move, and have our being'.

J.M.C.
St. Augustine
1987

CHAPTER ONE

INTRODUCTION

Computers can be physically linked via a communications channel to facilitate the sharing of hardware and software resources, and to allow the immediate and accurate transfer of information over distances ranging from less than a meter within a single room to thousands of kilometers across continents and over oceans. Such an arrangement also allows jobs and processes to be distributed to separate computers where they can be executed in parallel resulting in an increase in the number of jobs done in unit time. Issues which pertain both to the hardware and software design of such an interconnection of autonomous computers can generally be classified as *distributed computing*.

The demand for significant increases in computer processing speeds over those provided by uniprocessor systems has resulted in the design of single computer configurations containing many thousands of processing units. The parallelism in program execution is now not only at a job or process level, but has reached down to the point where individual machine instructions can be allocated to separate processors. The hardware and software issues pertaining to such single computer multiprocessor arrangements can generally be classified as *parallel computing*.

In this book, we will be looking at hardware organization and software design for distributed and parallel computing. We have made a distinction between distributed and parallel computing in order to reflect what seems to be the dominant view among the computer fraternity. One will still find instances, here and elsewhere, where these terms are used interchangeably. Indeed, it can be safely said that the computation can be distributed within a parallel computer environment, or that the distributed computing environment can be used to exploit the parallelism in some computation.

1

1.1 A BRIEF HISTORY

Computer technology developed comparatively slowly after Blaise Pascal's calculating machine appeared in 1642. Almost two centuries elapsed before Charles Babbage's difference engine (1812–1832) and analytical engine (1833–1871) were built. It took another century before the electromechanical computers of the late 1930s and early 1940s appeared. However, the pace of development quickened considerably after the creation of the first electronic computers in the 1940s and early 1950s. These initial electronic wonders were bulky, used large amounts of power and were often unreliable (Randell, 1975; Spencer, 1983).

These early systems could only be used by one person at a time. The development of the transistor and, shortly thereafter, integrated circuitry meant that less bulky, more powerful and more reliable computers could be built. It subsequently became apparent that single user uniprogramming operation was grossly inefficient.

Together with the development of the hardware, there was the development of software systems to manage these hardware resources with a view towards making more efficient use of the available computing power. Operating systems soon came on the scene. The earliest operating systems afforded only *batch stream operation*, where a number of jobs were placed in a *batch* of data cards which were then input to the computer. The operating system would then handle the batch by executing each job in turn (see Figure 1.1).

However, these batch systems, operating in a uniprogramming environment, did not make efficient use of the computer resources. The

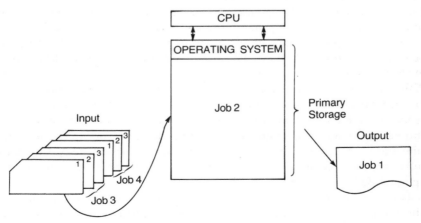

Fig. 1.1   Batch processing in a uniprogramming environment

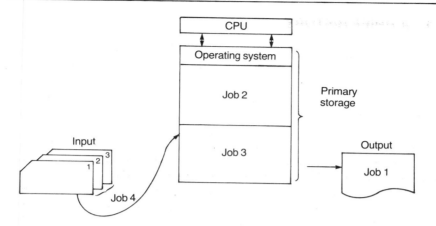

Fig. 1.2 Batch processing in a multiprogramming environment

great difference in speeds between the central processing unit (CPU) and the input/output peripherals resulted in poor use of the CPU, since there would often be significant CPU idle time while waiting on a slow peripheral. This led to the development of multiprogramming which allowed more than one program to be in execution at the same time (see Figure 1.2).

In the early single-user hands-on environment, *interactive* operation was possible, i.e. the programmer could examine and modify elements of the program during processing. Batch stream processing did not provide this interactive facility. However, there are applications which are better handled in an interactive mode. Therefore, with the development of key-input terminals and the necessary interrupt-driven operating systems, interactive programming was reintroduced. This soon led to another dimension in shared computer facilities.

Time-sharing systems, where more than one user can run programs on the computer from separate terminals at the same time were developed (see Figure 1.3). Such systems were in relatively common use by the early 1970s. It was soon possible to support *real-time* systems, where the computer was expected to respond to a query immediately, e.g. airline reservation systems, or monitor the operation of a physical process, e.g. temperature levels in a turbine. Although most of the computers used had only one CPU, multiprocessor systems were introduced into some environments to provide even more time-sharing and real-time capabilities.

Towards the end of the 1960s and during the early 1970s, two significant developments in the history of computing occurred. These developments: microprocessor technology and computer networking,

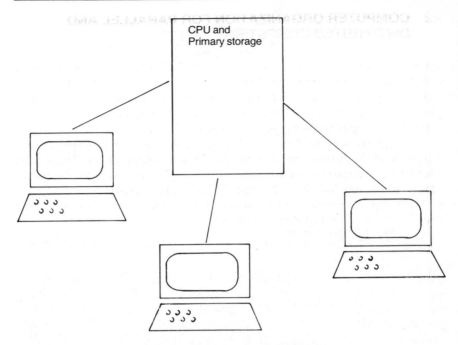

Fig. 1.3   Interactive terminal environment

opened up tremendous opportunities in the fields of computing and communication.

The great reduction in the size of computer processors, made possible by very large scale integrated circuitry, brought about a significant decrease in the cost of computer hardware. There has also been a vast increase in reliability. The versatility provided by these smaller components has made it possible to use microprocessors in many areas. Computer systems with thousands of processing elements constitute one of these areas. These systems now offer very many opportunities for parallel computing.

Communications technology is another of the areas that have benefited from microelectronics. We now have not only the home microcomputer but also the facility to link that home computer to other computers via communication networks (Davies and Barber, 1973; Davies et al, 1979). This has presented many avenues for processing and transferring information and the sharing of computer resources.

In the following sections we will open small windows to the areas of distributed and parallel computing that will be discussed in this text. Each section is expanded as a chapter.

1.2 COMPUTER ORGANIZATION FOR PARALLEL AND DISTRIBUTED COMPUTING

On-line access to many processors at the same time presents many opportunities for parallel and distributed computing. The computational task can be divided into several subtasks and different processors can be allocated to execute these subtasks. There must be some control to ensure that the participating processors cooperate.

A large class of problems for which computer-aided solutions are sought lend themselves to distribution. Indeed, in the area of large-scale scientific computations – aeronautics, nuclear physics, etc. – parallelism in processing seems like the only feasible way (Parter, 1984).

Different computer organizations have materialized to meet the demand for parallel and distributed computing:

(a) There are *multiprocessor systems* with a few processors which share a common memory.
(b) There are *massively parallel systems* with thousands of processing elements, where each element has a dedicated memory module.
(c) There are *multicomputer systems* which include computers each with its own private memory. These computers are connected via a high-speed communication link and are localized within a relatively small area (usually a single room).
(d) There are *computer networks* which link autonomous computers via a *communication network*.

Issues which arise when the computation is distributed include:

(a) how to achieve effective communication among the separate sub-tasks; and
(b) how to synchronize the subtask activity to ensure that the correct results are generated.

Parallel systems fall into a number of categories. There are systems which contain multiple processing elements capable of executing the *same* instruction on distinct sets of operands simultaneously. There are also systems with multiple processing elements each capable of executing a *different* instruction sequence simultaneously on distinct sets of operands. Furthermore, there are machines which can switch back and forth between these different modes of operation.

Multicomputers and computer networks permit many forms of distribution in the computation. The computational tasks can be categorized by type and different computers can be dedicated to perform particular types of functions. For example, I/O on slow peripherals could be distinguished from CPU intensive activity. Floating point computation could be distinguished from text editing, and so on.

On the other hand, processors may all handle the same type of job. The scheduling discipline may be designed so that it generates an equitable distribution of the processing load among the communicating processors.

In order to make good use of the parallel architecture, guidelines and tools for algorithm and program development must exist. We will look at this in Chapter 7 where we discuss parallel programming languages. However, we must observe here that the availability of techniques for constructing parallel algorithms serves as a strong motivation to build machines to perform the execution.

This has been the case in the design of some non von Neumann-type computers, namely *data-flow* and *reduction machines* (see section 2.5). A fundamentally different approach to program code formulation has stimulated research and development in this area.

1.3 COMMUNICATIONS AND COMPUTER NETWORKS

In Chapter 3 we will look at some communication principles and expand on the computer network, which was introduced in the previous section. Computer networks facilitate the exchange of information among computers. Expensive hardware resources, e.g. a high speed disk or high quality printer, and software resources, e.g. a database or large compiler can be shared among the users of the network.

There is the facility to access information at remote sites in negligible time. Processing tasks in a particular job may be distributed among sites thus using available computer power more efficiently. There is, too, the increased reliability provided by the availability of interconnected alternative resources in the event of an isolated breakdown. These capabilities all combine to produce better price/performance ratios in the operation of computer systems.

The computer network includes the computers on which the users run programs or applications. These computers are called *hosts*. These hosts are connected by a *communication subnet* of *communication processors*. The communication processors are usually referred to as *IMPs* (interface message processors) or *PSNs* (packet switch nodes) (see Figure 1.4). The subnet is the environment where the main communication functions are undertaken (Tanenbaum, 1981).

Networks are placed into two broad classes: wide area or long-haul networks (*WANs*) and local area networks (*LANs*). The wide area network covers a wide geographic area, even connecting continents whereas the LAN covers a small geographic area, e.g. an office block or university campus. LANs do not usually have a communication subnet.

Computer network development has benefited significantly from the pioneering work done by *ARPA* (Advanced Research Projects Agency) of the U.S. Department of Defense (now called DARPA). They gave us

ARPANET in the late 1960s, on which many fundamental issues have been tried and tested, and from where many network terms (e.g., IMP) have originated (Tanenbaum, 1981).

Designers must address several communication issues. These include:

(a) the quantity and quality of information that the **communication link** can carry;
(b) the choice of suitable communication media from the many alternatives that exist;
(c) the sharing of the **communication channel** among the many competing users; and
(d) the development and maintenance of an acceptable level of reliability in the transfer of information.

Modularity in design has always been recommended as a sensible approach to systems design. This has been the case in the building of computer networks. The architecture involves a number of layers, each layer being implemented at all the hosts. The layers must range from the hardware level to the user level. Each layer will then behave as if it is communicating only with the corresponding layer at the other sites. Guidelines must be established to permit this layer-to-layer communication. Such guidelines are usually referred to as **protocols**.

Therefore the situation that obtains between two hosts is as follows:

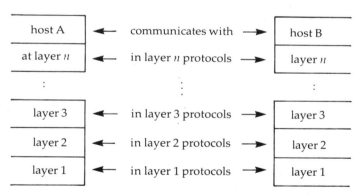

The actual transfer of information occurs only at the lowest layer, i.e. the physical layer.

In addition to matters of architecture, there are also matters of topology. This covers matters concerning where to locate the computers and how to link them together so as to minimize cost and at the same time achieve acceptable performance levels.

Multiprocessor and multicomputer systems are designed to afford distribution of computation across many processing elements. Computer networks have extended this capability and have opened the way to many new and exciting applications.

IDPC—B

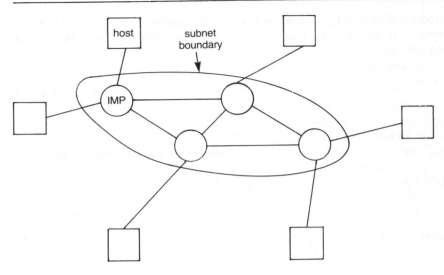

Fig. 1.4   Schematic of a computer network

Some applications are *file transfer, electronic mail* and *electronic funds transfer*, the accessing of remote databases, and the automated office. There are social implications which follow from the proliferation of network facilities. Think of the difference in lifestyle already afforded by public information networks, home banking systems and being able to work on the office mainframe without traveling many kilometers to the office.

In order to support these and other distributed applications, a reliable software environment must be designed, implemented and maintained. This environment will include programs and data structures which can be considered as essential features of distributed computing.

1.4   OPERATING SYSTEMS FOR DISTRIBUTED AND PARALLEL COMPUTING

In a computing environment where many computers or processors are linked, the operating system has to present the user with the facilities for parallelism or distribution in as friendly a manner as possible. A desirable objective, therefore, is to create an interface with the system which allows that user to feel that his or her interactions are with a single computer or processor.

The vehicle for user interaction with the computer system is the command language. The user sees the system through this command language. The operating system must provide commands which give the users access to the facilities. It may be helpful if the users do not have to specify in the command the separate processors that will be involved in handling the users' tasks.

In computer networks, each host computer runs its own operating system. These operating systems can fall into one of two categories.

(a) They can be cooperating similar local editions of one large homogeneous operating system. This arrangement is classified as a *distributed operating system*. Such systems are more likely to be found in networks which use highly compatible machinery, i.e. all the computers may be from the same manufacturer.

(b) They can be distinct heterogeneous operating systems which co-operate through network-access *agent processes*. Such systems can easily accommodate the differences in machine design prevalent in wide area networks. This arrangement is usually classified as a *network operating system*.

One of the major issues in operating system design that is particularly relevant to distributed computing is the implementation of a communication mechanism for process-to-process interaction. Whatever the system proposed, there should be easy extension from purely local interaction to interaction with remote systems.

This need to accommodate easy extension to foreign sites has helped to bring the designers to the drawing boards to develop efficient interprocess communication schemes at the kernel level. A communication system can also provide synchronization of activity among processes. Processes can be forced to wait on each other for explicit responses before moving on to anything else. On the other hand, messages can be deposited with no waiting.

The control of access to shared resources continues to be of major importance. The linking of a facility to a communications network exposes that facility, in many cases, to a large user base. With that domain of users, there is always the probability (sometimes a high one) that malicious intruders exist.

In parallel computing the operating system must manage the many processing units and other resources which are available efficiently. The parallel strands within the program have to be identified, they must be allocated to available units, and their interactions ought to be adequately controlled.

These are the areas that we will look at in more detail in Chapter 4.

1.5 SERVERS IN A CLIENT-SERVER MODEL

The linking of computers in a network makes the services that are located at single sites widely available. One of the strongest arguments for a computer network is the opportunity to share services in this way. In many cases, the cost of an expensive resource, like a large fixed disk or laser printer, cannot be justified if its use is restricted to one department.

The *client-server model* of distributed computing identifies the service and provides a software system to administer that service. This software system includes:

(a) the *server* which 'produces' the service and usually runs on a dedicated computer that owns the resource being used; and
(b) the *clients* which 'consume' the service being provided and run on the user machines.

Some examples of server systems are *file servers*, *printer servers* and *name servers*. The file server allows shared file storage facilities, the printer server allows the sharing of a printer, and the name server maintains a directory of named services so that these services can be located in an efficient manner. File server systems seem to be the most popular of such systems. This can be easily appreciated in the light of the considerable significance of file storage and retrieval facilities in information systems.

Security considerations arise again here. Although the objective is to increase the availability of the resource, there has to be adequate control to ensure only authorized use. Furthermore, there are several communication matters that must be handled. Individual requests for service must be identifiable. The server must be able to determine that it has already handled a particular request. A client should be able to repeat a request when it assumes that an earlier one was not received. The client must be satisfied that his request has been handled.

The server should not be swamped by unexpectedly heavy demands by clients. There must be the facility to regulate this flow of traffic. In order to improve throughput times, concurrent access is allowed. However, this can generate inconsistent data areas. Some mechanism must be employed to ensure that data areas, when changed, preserve the integrity of the information that is stored.

1.6   DISTRIBUTED DATABASE SYSTEMS

Database systems provide a central storage facility for all operational data of an organization and allow information retrieval pertaining to the various application needs of that organization. For example, both the marketing and the production departments need to look at items in stock. Hence, a single stock file can be shared between these two departments. The database removes the requirement for each department to store its own copy of those data items, i.e. unnecessary redundancies can be avoided. Some redundancy is necessary in order to facilitate recovery from failures. If there is no back-up copy then there will be nothing to revert to in some crisis situations.

With the advent of computer networks the computer facilities at separate branches of the same organisation can be linked. The question which now arises is, What is the best way in which the operational data can be distributed? Since the database system has been shown to be effective for information storage and retrieval, any distribution must preserve the database concept.

An alternative to this is to centralize the database and force all the remote branches to access the database through the network. This is, perhaps, the simplest system to implement but it may offer reduced reliability and availability. Failures at the central site affect all the sites. Responses to remote queries are subject to all the difficulties which arise in the communication system. Furthermore, there is the matter of communication cost which most certainly must be considered.

Every site can be allowed to store a database to meet its dominant needs and still have remote access to other sites when the need arises. In this arrangement, we will have a number of cooperating databases forming a network-wide *distributed database system*. An example of such a system can be taken from the banking sector. Each bank branch can maintain a local database of accounts on its customers and these component databases can cooperate to facilitate on-line account entries from remote branches.

There are other ways in which the distribution of the operational data can be done. Infrequently referenced fragments may be stored at a single site while those which are more frequently referenced may be copied everywhere to increase availability. There is more redundancy in this system, but it has to be weighed against the benefits that will be derived from the quicker response.

In a distributed database system, alternatives may exist in the way in which a query is handled. That is, the data elements that are needed may be duplicated at different sites. This means that there is a choice among sites from which to obtain data and at which to perform the operations. This leads to considerations on how to optimize query processing with a view to minimizing cost. This cost arises both in the on-site processing operations and the communication load generated.

Another matter that is of prime concern is ensuring that all the copies of the database segments are always consistently updated. Updates to one copy must be successfully propagated throughout the database within an acceptable time frame. Users must never be allowed to see an incorrect picture.

Recovery problems are more complex than in the centralized database. Not only must there be support mechanisms at the local site to facilitate recovery, but the communication protocols must be designed to accommodate failure gracefully.

1.7 PARALLEL PROGRAMMING LANGUAGES

The predominant body of programming languages support only sequential processing. This constitutes a serious disincentive to software designers who would like to utilize the distributed and parallel facilities that are increasingly becoming available. Fortunately, there have been some attempts to correct this imbalance and so allow the software development to get in step with the strides in hardware.

A parallel language provides data and control structures for expressing the inherent parallelism of the problem being tackled. This reduces and, for some tasks, removes the need to think at the hardware level when coding. However, it must be added at this point that some systems' programming tasks will require low-level control which is not provided in most of these parallel programming languages; hence, it will still be necessary to program, at times, in a language which allows this machine control. This discussion will be amplified in Chapter 7.

Many of the parallel language projects form part of larger distributed projects. It follows, therefore, that there are instances where the language may be architecture-specific as in the case of a language for an array processor. However, there are others which are aimed at a larger user base.

Important issues are the identification and specification of the parallel streams of activity within a program, the communication among the parallel streams and the synchronization of the activity as required by the characteristics of the problem.

There are also those languages which provide a non von Neumann-style of computation. In the von Neumann framework, there is a stored program comprising a list of instructions. These instructions usually cause the manipulation of named memory locations called variables. The program counter indicates the next instruction to be executed. This execution involves fetching of the instruction, interpreting the operation, fetching operands, performing the function, then storing the results.

The non von Neumann systems have emerged from work in *functional programming* and *data-flow* languages. In functional languages, there is a progressive application of functions to arguments. This means that the entire program must be expressed as a combination of defined functions. A reference to a function demands its application to the arguments supplied. The execution of a function is determined by the nature of the problem and the availability of a processor. Parallel machines can be designed to support this system.

Data-flow incorporates graphs to represent the computation path that should be followed in solving the problem. One can think in terms of a very detailed flowchart where the nodes are the individual instructions and the arcs are the individual operands. The availability of operands forces the performance of the operation. Parallel systems can be designed to accommodate the data-flow mechanism. Individual operations can be associated with distinct processing elements.

1.8 SUMMARY

Computers have developed from mechanical systems with very limited capabilities to the electronic wonders of our time with capabilities that were almost unimaginable thirty years ago. Systems with massively parallel features are now available. In addition to job and process level parallelism, opportunities now exist for instruction level distribution of the computation.

The merging of communications and computing has produced a revolution in information technology that is affecting our very lifestyle. Many new application areas have been created through the availability of computer networks. Computer networking technology began in the late 1960s and there are now many operational wide and local area networks. A layered architecture has been adopted in network design and protocols describe how communication should be done at each layer and across layer boundaries.

A reliable and efficient software environment has to be constructed to provide an acceptable level of service to the users of distributed and parallel computing facilities. In addressing this area, several different streams of software activity have emerged. Some examples of these streams are network and distributed operating systems, client-server systems, distributed database systems and parallel language design projects.

1.9 QUESTIONS

1.1 One of the objectives in building parallel systems is increased processing speeds. Suggest some reasons for the ever present desire to obtain faster processing rates.

1.2 Computer networks provide opportunities for the exchange of information and the sharing of resources. Suggest some reasons why, in spite of these privileges, there might be some reluctance to hook one's computer facility onto a communications network.

1.3 Indicate some of the key issues in the design of an operating system for distributed computing.

1.4 Assume that you are the manager of a computer center for a large university. There is a local computer network with access points throughout the university campus. You have just added an expensive document preparation facility to the network. Suggest some mechanisms that you could implement to restrict its use to a small group of privileged users.

1.5 Suggest an organization other than the banking industry that you think can benefit from a distributed database system. Comment on the ways in which the distribution of the data could be done and the advantages and disadvantages which will arise.

1.6 'The design of parallel programming languages can serve as an impetus for the building of parallel computers, as well as it can be motivated by the availability of such machines.' Discuss.

1.10 REFERENCES

1 Davies, D.W. and Barber, D.L.A., 1973. *Communication Networks for Computers.* London: John Wiley & Sons.
2 Davies, D.W., Barber, D.L.A., Price, W.L. and Solomonides, C.M., 1979. *Computer Networks and their Protocols.* Chichester: John Wiley & Sons.
3 Parter, S.V. (ed.), 1984. *Large Scale Scientific Computation.* Orlando, Fa.: Academic Press, Inc.
4 Randell, B. (ed.), 1975. *The Origins of Digital Computers, Selected papers, 2nd edition.* Berlin: Springer-Verlag.
5 Spencer, D.D., 1983. *An Introduction to Computers.* Ohio: Charles E. Merrill Pub. Co.
6 Tanenbaum, A.S., 1981. *Computer Networks.* Englewood Cliffs, N.J.: Prentice Hall.

CHAPTER TWO

COMPUTER ORGANIZATION FOR PARALLEL AND DISTRIBUTED COMPUTING

A computer program can be described as the specification of some number of computational procedures. These procedures are usually executed sequentially due to at least one of the following reasons:

(a) there is only one central processing unit;
(b) the logic of the program is sequential; or
(c) the programming language permits only a sequential flow of instructions.

Uniprocessor multiprogramming systems allow concurrent processing where the sequence of instructions executed may include subsets of instructions from unrelated procedures or processes (see Figure 2.1). However, the mode of execution remains serial.

This is the way in which many of us still have our jobs done. We feed them into some mini or medium mainframe uniprocessor where they are multiprogrammed in this *context-switching* manner. Of course, there are scheduling policies which dictate who gets the processor and sometimes these policies do not serve everyone's best interest.

Many computing tasks can be subdivided into distinct procedures (or processes) which can be done simultaneously, i.e. in a parallel mode. For example, let us assume the following computation is to be performed:

$$B(I) = A(I) * A(I) + SQRT(A(I)) \text{ for } I = 1 \ldots N,$$

where 'SQRT' is the square root function. Here we have a squaring process and a square root process being done on the same operands. There would be increased throughput if the operations:

$$C(I) = A(I) * A(I),$$

15

and

$$D(I) = SQRT(A(I))$$

could be allocated to different processors and therefore be run at the same time. Hence, it is desirable to have computers with many processors among which the computation can be distributed.

A computational task can be distributed among geographically dispersed computers which are either located close to the data source or are ideally suited, by virtue of some hardware or software resource, to perform some aspect of the computation. Linking these computers via a communications network can provide effective on-line processing and control.

For example, the point-of-sale terminals distributed over a chain of outlets of a large departmental store can compute the total purchase for each customer, update the local branch's inventory, and through a communication link to a central computer, can provide timely sales information for management planning and control.

In another environment, there could be a powerful 'number crunching' machine to do the floating point computations, another machine to do the text editing, and a third to handle the final document or report preparation.

Many large-scale scientific and engineering applications, e.g. digital signal and image processing, computer vision, large-scale simulation, knowledge-based systems, etc., contain procedures that can be executed in parallel. In some cases, it is only by exploiting this parallelism that undertaking such projects becomes feasible.

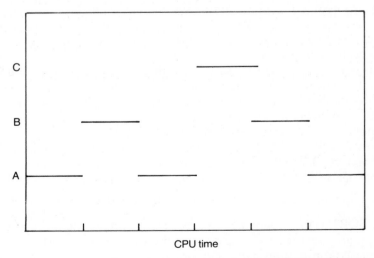

CPU time

Fig. 2.1 Concurrent processing of processes A, B and C in a uniprocessor environment

The amount of time that will be consumed if these applications were implemented in a serial mode constitutes a serious constraint. Indeed, it has been observed (Hoshino et al, 1983) that the numerical simulation of large-scale technological systems like nuclear fusion devices and supersonic wind tunnels requires computing speeds at least a thousand times faster than the available uniprocessor systems.

The available technology limits the power of the single processor. Furthermore, the physical laws which govern the behavior of electronic components place an ultimate limit on the speed of the processing unit. Hence, for significantly increased computing power, it is advisable to build systems which permit parallel processing or some overlap in instruction execution.

In the sections which follow systems which allow a departure from that strict sequential mode of processing will be introduced. These include *pipeline machines*, *multicomputers*, *computer networks* and *multiprocessors*. The availability of fast and relatively cheap microprocessors and large memory capacities has provided opportunities for building massively parallel systems. Such systems are best considered under *parallel architecture*. Finally we will look at projects involving *non von Neumann-type* parallel machines.

2.1 PIPELINE AND VECTOR PROCESSORS

One approach used to provide faster computation is the building of pipeline processors, which permit overlap in the execution of instructions. The pipeline concept involves the division of an instruction into a number of distinct stages, each of which can be allocated to a separate processing unit. A good illustration of the pipeline system is the operation of an automobile assembly line: at one point in the line the welding is done, at another there is the painting, and so on.

Some of the stages into which an instruction can be divided are:

(a) fetching the instruction;
(b) decoding it;
(c) calculating the effective address of the operands;
(d) obtaining the operands;
(e) executing the operation; and
(f) returning the result to store.

If an independent processing unit is allocated to each of these six stages, then a maximum of six instructions, each at a different stage, can be handled at the same time. When the first has reached stage 6, the second will be at stage 5, the third at stage 4 and so on.

Since the particular operation to be performed can differ, e.g. an add operation, a subtract operation, etc, then at some point in the pipeline there has to be the determination of which execution unit is to be involved. Time will be saved if it is determined beforehand that there is a long sequence of the same instruction. For example consider the computation,

$$C(I) = A(I) + B(I), I = 1,2,\ldots N; \text{ for large } N.$$

N additions are required and therefore there will be N activations of the *decode* or *interpret* unit, each indicating that an 'add' is involved. On the other hand, there could be the facility to make a single interpretation and also obtain the number, N, of such operations to be performed. Hence, the whole sequence can initially be allocated to the same path through the pipeline. In this case, there will be a saving of $N - 1$ decode operations. Pipeline processors which incorporate this facility to execute the same instruction on a vector of operands is called a *vector processor*.

Examples of pipeline machines include the IBM 360/195, the University of Manchester MU5, the CDC Star 100, the Cyber 205, the FPS 5105, the CRAY-1 and CRAY-2 (Garside, 1980; Gorsline, 1986). Such machines have met some of the demands for increased processing power. Let us take a brief look at the CRAY-1.

The CRAY-1 was built for the specific purpose of processing vectors. However, there are also scalar operations in its 104 instruction set.

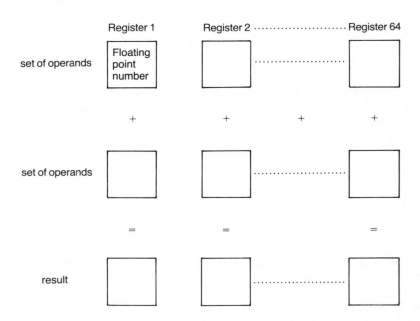

Fig. 2.2   Two sets of 64 floating point numbers can be added in one vector add in the CRAY-1

A single vector add instruction can add together two sets of 64 bit floating point operands where each set contains 64 individual elements each stored in a register. Therefore, we have one vector add generating 64 pipelined additions (see Figure 2.2).

A vector operation can consume from 2 to 14 suboperations in the pipeline. Each suboperation takes 12.5 ns. Therefore, after pipe-fill, i.e. $12.5*14$, where 14 suboperations are necessary, vector elements of the result can be obtained at intervals of 12.5 ns.

For example, a portion of a timing chart for the vector addition

$$C(I) = A(I) + B(I), \text{ for } I = 1 \ldots N,$$

where we assume that 6 suboperations are necessary, would look like the following:

A(1),B(1)→(12.5ns) →(12.5ns) →(12.5ns) →...→(12.5ns) →C(1)
         sub-op 1   sub-op 2   sub-op 3 . . .   sub-op 6

    A(2),B(2)→(12.5ns) →(12.5ns) →(12.5ns) →. . . (12.5ns) →C(2)
             sub-op 1   sub-op 2   sub-op 3 . . .   sub-op 6

        A(3),B(3)→(12.5ns) →(12.5ns) →(12.5ns) →
                   sub-op 1   sub-op 2   sub-op 3

    . . . (12.5ns) →C(3)
    . . . sub-op 6

A pair of operands from a set of 64 pairs will enter the pipe every 12.5 ns. Where N is less than 64, the set will equal that number. If N is greater than 64, there will be looping until completion.

This computer is quite suitable for problems involving the numerical modeling of the behavior of physical systems like fluid, the weather and seismic activity.

2.2 MULTICOMPUTERS AND COMPUTER NETWORKS

Multicomputers and computer networks consist of separate processors with their own private memories. These are sometimes described as *loosely coupled* systems. Both of these arrangements employ a number of computers physically linked to permit on-line computer-to-computer communications.

The multicomputer system extends over a distance of not more than a few meters within the same room or building. The physical connection is usually via a bus or channel that permits parallel stream transmission of data. In a parallel transmission scheme, a byte or word is transmitted with each bit traveling along a separate line within the bus and arriving at the same time. Parallel transmission of a byte can be compared to eight cars (one for each bit) traveling abreast along an eight lane highway.

The computer network can extend over vast distances restricted only by the available communications facility. The transmission system is serial. When a byte is transmitted, the bits are sent one after the other along the same line. Computer networks usually employ signal conversion techniques in order to make use of existing communication systems like the public telephone network. Computer networks will be discussed in some detail in Chapter 3.

The multicomputer system has transmission speeds almost comparable with the rate of the processors. Furthermore, as a result of the close proximity of the processors, there can be a high degree of connectivity and a very low incidence of transmission errors.

Because the distance between processors is small, the transmission cannot suffer the extent of noise interference as in the case of the wider communication network. In addition, the problem of *skew* in parallel stream transmission is immaterial. Skew refers to the failure of a number of bits to arrive in parallel even though they are transmitted in parallel (see Figure 2.3). Small differences in the characteristics of the individual communication lines along which the bits travel cause this skew. It follows that this problem is aggravated as the distance increases.

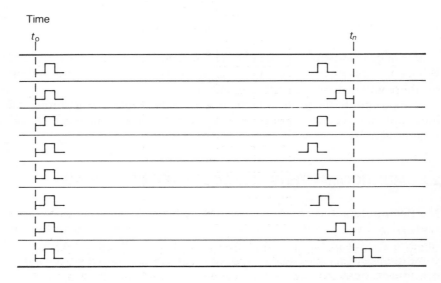

Fig. 2.3 The effect of skewing in parallel transmission of bits

Furthermore, multiple paths can be set up between computers. In fact, there could be a fully connected network (i.e., all possible physical links exist) allowing a high degree of fault tolerance. However, in many cases there are only two computers involved and they communicate via a shared peripheral I/O device or some common memory module.

A multicomputer can be used to distribute processing by type e.g., computation can be assigned to one computer while input/output processing can be assigned to another. In the 1960s, there was the multicomputer arrangement involving the IBM 1401 and the IBM 7090 computers. The IBM 1401 handled the card reader to tape, tape to printer and tape to card punch peripheral transfers for the IBM 7090, which did its I/O on the tape devices only. Initially, there was manual tape fetching between the IBM 1401 and the 7090 tape drives. However, this was soon

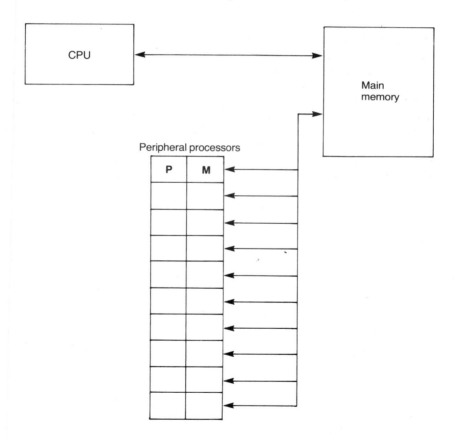

Fig. 2.4 A schematic of the CDC 6600 multicomputer organization. P stands for processor and M for memory. Harold Lorin, *Parallelism in Hardware and Software: Real and Apparent Concurrency*, © 1972, p. 181. Adapted by permission of Prentice Hall Inc., Englewood Cliffs, New Jersey

upgraded to allow both computers to be physically linked to the same tape drive.

A later configuration was the IBM *attached support processor* (ASP) system. In this system, two computers from the IBM 360 series (and later the 370 series) were linked via a high speed channel. One computer, the ASP, was dedicated to peripheral activity, while the larger computer served as the main processor.

Another significant main/peripheral multicomputer is the CDC 6600. It contains one large CPU for computation and ten *peripheral processors*. Each peripheral processor has its own relatively small private memory, while the main memory belongs to the large CPU (see Figure 2.4). The peripheral processors can all transfer data to and from the main memory, by which means interprocessor communication is afforded (Garside, 1980; Gorsline, 1986).

In the computer network environment, this separation of I/O activity from computational activity, is one example of what is called the *client-server* model of distribution. Computers in a network are dedicated to perform certain service functions and when a user's task requires such service, the appropriate processor or computer is called. Several computers can be allowed to share the same disk drive for the storage and retrieval of files. This file service will be managed by a dedicated computer called the *file server*. The client-server model is discussed in more detail in Chapter 5.

The computation can also be distributed among processors in order to regulate the work load. A processor must not be overloaded if there are other processors available to accommodate an increased load. This arrangement assumes that all the processors have predominantly similar characteristics and are, therefore, suitable to handle similar tasks. Better throughput times can be achieved if the load is evenly spread. In order to achieve this, an appropriate scheduling scheme has to be implemented.

One approach is to allocate the scheduling task to one processor (a master) which would distribute the tasks to the other processors (the slaves) in accordance with some scheduling algorithm. For example, the slave processors may be arranged logically in a circular list for process assignment. The master accesses the process queue and allocates a process to the next idle slave in the circle.

This arrangement can be modified in a small way to accommodate multiple master/slave relationships. The processors are divided into groups with each group having a master responsible for the group scheduling. There can also be an extension to a tree arrangement where there is a single grandmaster responsible for the scheduling of the group masters. However this extension may not be attractive since the whole system becomes tied to the performance of the grandmaster at the root.

On the other hand, a pool of processors connected via a network may all hold equal status, i.e. no master/slave arrangement. A job may originate

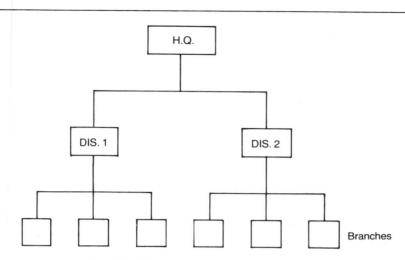

Fig. 2.5 Hierarchical distribution of computation

on any processor and as a process is created, its attributes – amount of memory, text or floating-point intensive, etc. – are broadcast to the other processors. Processors willing to run the process must submit bids (Tanenbaum, 1981) from which the creating processor makes a selection. This arrangement is more complex to manage and therefore there is a greater possibility of *deadlocks*.

A hierarchical arrangement of computers can be used to match the hierarchical relationship among the processing functions of a large organization. Processing tasks at individual plants or branches can be handled by local computers which can also channel information via the communications net to district level computers to meet processing requirements at that level. Furthermore, there can be a processing unit at the headquarters for top level management information systems (see Figure 2.5).

The large multinational corporations and other business conglo-merates are suitable candidates for such a hierarchical arrangement. Many business conglomerates comprise a group of companies which are under the umbrella of a central holding company. Each subsidiary company in the group can have a number of branches managed by that company's headquarters, which in turn reports to the central holding company. Computerization can reflect this structure.

2.3 MULTIPROCESSORS

The *multiprocessor* system can be viewed as one computer with a global primary storage area shared by all the processors. This system is sometimes regarded as being *tightly coupled*. Whereas the earliest tightly coupled systems may hardly have exceeded ten processors, recent significant advances in *very large scale integrated circuitry* (VLSI) have brought about projects involving thousands of processors. These massively parallel systems will be discussed in the following section. In this section, our attention will be restricted to smaller systems.

These tightly coupled systems are controlled by a single operating system with each processor having access to a single job queue. Two of the issues that must be given special consideration are:

(a) the synchronization of interprocessor activity; and
(b) interprocessor communication.

2.3.1 Synchronization

Adequate processor synchronization mechanisms must be employed to ensure acceptable levels of performance. If two processors have access to the same process queue, the selection of the same process by both processors as well as the omission of a process by both processors are cases that should be prevented. Both cases can arise if the updating done by the processors to the pointer to 'next-process' is not properly coordinated.

Processors may cooperate in the execution of a single job. Separate processes of the same job may be allocated to different processors. There may, therefore, be some order which the execution of these processes must follow. For example, given that process A must select the ten most frequently occurring real numbers from an array which contains more than ten distinct real numbers and process B must find the average of the ten numbers selected it is difficult to see how the correct results can be obtained if process B is executed before process A. Hence it is necessary that processor activity be synchronized correctly.

Furthermore, since the processors are all accessing common operating system modules there can be serious contention for these resources. Some of this contention can be reduced if the processor clocks are skewed. This would ensure that interrupts from different processors cannot occur at the same time. This facility is used in DEC's Symmetrical Multiprocessing (SMP) system. In addition, there will be the need to implement some software locking mechanism to provide a greater level of control.

Useful mutual exclusion and synchronization routines are discussed in many of the fundamental texts on operating systems (see Deitel, 1984; Peterson and Silberschatz, 1983). These issues will be discussed in some detail in Chapter 4 where we look at operating systems and in Chapter 7 where we look at parallel programming languages.

2.3.2 Interprocessor communication

Interprocessor communication mechanisms must be implemented to

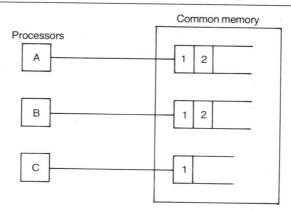

Fig. 2.6 Multiprocessor system with buffers for interprocessor communication

facilitate the coordination of computational activity. Individual processors may be allocated separate memory areas to act as message buffers for information transfer between processors. For example, if the processors have specific functions, then the operating system may, on identifying a particular procedure, create a process and indicate to the appropriate processor that the process exists by appending a message to that processor's queue (see Figure 2.6).

In DEC's TOPS-10 SMP system, processors share a common memory but each processor has its own I/O devices. A processor can be running a program that requests I/O on a device that belongs to a different processor. Therefore, each processor has its own I/O queues to which are appended its own I/O requests as well as those from other processors.

In a multiprocessing system there will be times when a processor has no productive work. There may not be enough work to go around, hence a processor can be in an idle state. Such a processor must be signaled when there is work to be done. The SIGP command (signal processor) on the IBM System/370 provides this capability. One processor can 'shoulder tap' another processor by issuing an SIGP command, thus generating immediate response on some task. Another technique is to demand that the idle processor 'listen' for a signal which indicates that its services are needed. This approach is used in DEC's SMP.

There has to be some underlying physical interconnection system to support the communication among the processors. Some basic interconnection schemes that have been used are time shared or common buses, crossbar switch, multiport-memory system, and multistage networks (Enslow, 1977; Hwang and Briggs, 1984).

Time shared or common buses

In this arrangement, a single cable with enough lines to convey data and control bits acts as a passive channel to which all of the processors, I/O devices and memory modules are connected (see Figure 2.7). The interface

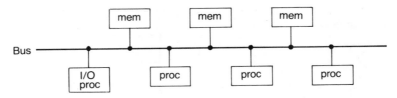

Fig. 2.7   Time shared or common bus multiprocessor arrangement

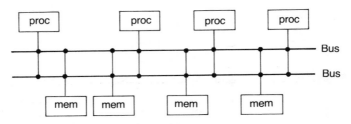

Fig. 2.8   A multibus multiprocessor arrangement

hardware between the bus and the functional units control the data transmission across the bus. With this single bus system, only one unit can use the medium at a time. Hence some mechanism must be introduced to resolve the contention for the use of the bus.

Although this is a simple, reliable and relatively inexpensive inter-connection network, the performance of the entire multiprocessor system now hinges on this single cable. One approach to improving the performance of the system is to increase the capability of the bus system. This can be done by providing multiple bidirectional buses (see Figure 2.8).

Crossbar switch

The number of buses may be increased to permit a separate path to each memory module, as in Figure 2.9. This arrangement is called a *crossbar switch.* Simultaneous transmissions for all the memory units are thus supported. This increased transmission capacity must, however, be weighed against the complexity that has been introduced in order to permit the switching at the crosspoints. This is compounded by the need to resolve multiple attempts at access to the same memory module.

Multiport memory system

Another multiple bus arrangement can be employed to allow processor access to the memory modules at a specific entry point called a *port* (see Figure 2.10). The switching and control intelligence of the system no longer resides at the crosspoints, but at the memory ports themselves.

The interconnection system is determined by the number and type of

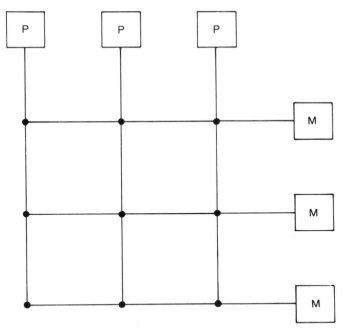

Fig. 2.9 A crossbar switch of three processors and three memory modules

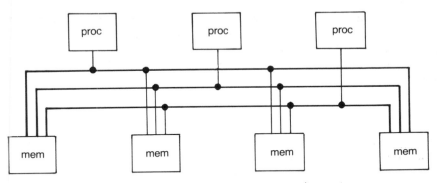

Fig. 2.10 A multiport memory interconnection system

memory ports available. This number may vary over the memory modules, and, indeed, a module could be exclusively allocated to a particular processor by dedicating its single port to accesses from that processor.

In order to support a large multiprocessor system, it is necessary to have a large number of cables and connectors. This is not an encouraging factor and, furthermore, once the number and type of ports are settled, there is little room for altering the configuration.

Multistage networks

The multistage network links multiple switches as nodes in a treelike arrangement. Figure 2.11 shows a tree of two-by-two switching nodes connecting two processors to eight memory modules. Each switch has the capacity to connect any one of its two inputs to any one of its two output lines.

The unused inputs at the second and lowest levels of the tree in Figure 2.11 can be used to build a fully configured multistage network with eight processors each having a unique path to each memory module (see Figure 2.12).

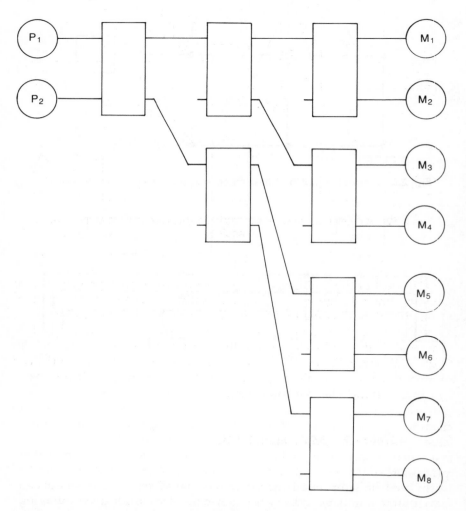

Fig. 2.11 A tree of two-by-two switching nodes connecting two processors to eight memory modules

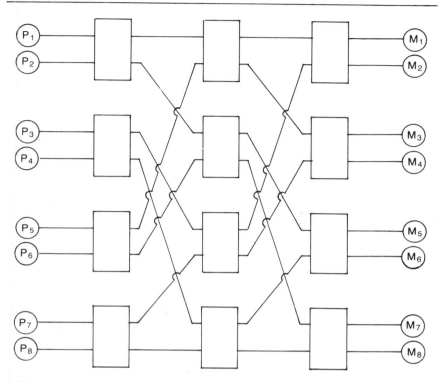

Fig. 2.12 A multistage network connecting eight processors to eight memory modules

The cost of the multistage network which connects n processors to n memory modules grows as $n \log n$. This differs somewhat considerably from that of the crossbar switch whose cost grows as n^2. The base of the log is the number of arcs fanning out of the node (two in our example). While the cost of the multistage is less than that of the crossbar switch, the potential for parallel access remains the same. However, contention can be more of a problem, although this can be offset by introducing extra pathways at the relatively lower cost.

2.4 PARALLEL ARCHITECTURE

The availability of relatively cheap and efficient microprocessors has produced a tremendous upsurge in the development of parallel computers. These computers now consist of numerous (up to thousands of) processors. These processors usually have reduced instruction sets and are frequently referred to as *processing elements* (PEs). Some of these parallel computers are designed to exploit parallelism in computation down to the level of individual instructions.

Although there is some work in progress on general-purpose models, the major interest seems to be in the area of specialized problems such as image processing, simulation of physical continua, etc. We will look at some of the models that exist and in a few instances refer to actual implementations.

2.4.1 Associative processors

Associative processors are designed to speed up the search for data items held in memory. The traditional method for obtaining an item from memory is via its address. Let us suppose that we were looking for the word 'JOEL' in the following memory block:

word 100	ANNA
101	BETH
102	DAWN
103	JOEL
104	VALE

There must first be the association of JOEL with some address at which the search must begin, i.e. an entry point to the memory block. Let that be *word 100*. Then follows a progressive fetching as the address is incremented up to *word 103* before there is a match on JOEL. In searching for a given item, many memory locations may have to be searched sequentially before there is a match.

An associative memory architecture permits the simultaneous searching of the whole of memory using the contents of a word, not its address, as the argument. The associative memory allows the use of JOEL as the search tool directly.

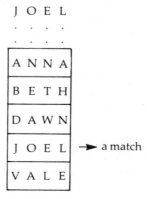

With the aid of associative processors a parallel examination of all the words in memory can be made to determine if there is a match on all (or some of) the bits in a word (see Figure 2.13). In the example above, the bit formation in JOEL is compared simultaneously with all the words in the memory block, and an indication is made where there is a match.

This system can be used as an index. The associative memory can contain the primary keys of data records held in nonassociative storage.

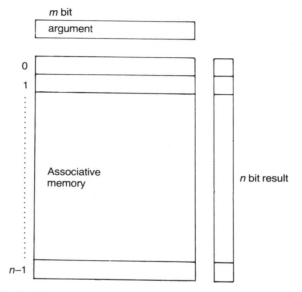

Fig. 2.13 Each of the *n* words are searched in parallel for a match. A '1' bit in the corresponding location in the result area can indicate a match

The location of the primary key in the associative storage can be a relative address of the data record, e.g. the *n*th entry in the associative memory is the primary key of the data record with relative address *n*. Given a primary key, a parallel search of the index can be made to determine the address of the data record.

The Goodyear Aerospace STARAN computer is an example of an associative processor system. It has 256 single bit processing elements which provide the ability to simultaneously search 256 bits (rowwise or columnwise) of 256 by 256 bit arrays. This machine can also simultaneously write into selected bit positions along a row or column (Gorsline, 1986).

2.4.2 Array processors (SIMD)

A set of identical processing elements synchronized to perform the same intruction simultaneously on different data is usually referred to as an

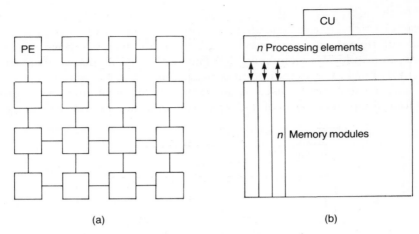

Fig. 2.14   (a) A nearest neighbor mesh
(b) An array processor organization

array processor. The PEs are usually organized as an array of processors connected in a *nearest neighbor mesh* network (see Figure 2.14a), i.e. each PE has a direct link with its nearest neighbors.

Array processors are classified after Flynn (1966) as *single instruction, multiple data-stream* (SIMD) computers. A typical configuration includes a set of n processors, n memory modules, an interconnection network and a control unit (see Figure 2.14b).

The control unit sends the instructions to the PEs. There is the facility to restrict the number of PEs that would execute an instruction, hence PEs can be *masked* at any time. Each enabled (not masked) PE will execute the instruction using data obtained from its private memory module. Inter-process communication takes places via the interconnection network.

The nearest neighbor mesh could be enhanced by connecting the first element of a row or column to the last element of that row or column as in Figure 2.15. A *cube network* could be used. A three-dimensional cube is shown in Figure 2.16a where each vertex is a node and the arcs or edges are the physical communication links. There are 8 nodes which can be numbered 0 to 7, thus each node can be represented by a 3-digit binary address. Hence we can call it a binary 3-cube. It has 2^3 nodes.

This cube concept can be extended to n dimensions giving an n-cube with 2^n nodes. The communication links can be determined from the routing function:

$$C_i(a_{n-1} \ldots a_1 a_0) = a_{n-1} \ldots a_{i+1}\bar{a}_i a_{i-1} \ldots a_0 \text{ for } i = 0, 1, \ldots n-1$$

where $a_{n-1} \ldots a_1 a_0$ is the n-bit address of the node and $\bar{a}_i$ is the complement of bit a_i.

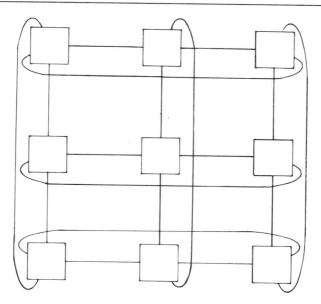

Fig. 2.15   A three-by-three nearest neighbor mesh (NNM) with end around connection

For example, when this routing function is applied to the node 101 in the 3-cube we get the following

$$C_0(101) = 100$$
$$C_1(101) = 111$$
$$C_2(101) = 001$$

as is denoted in Figure 2.16a.

Figure 2.16b shows a partial two dimensional projection of a binary 6-cube. As an exercise you can use the routing function to complete the interconnection.

ILLIAC-IV, ICL DAP, MMP and The Connection Machine

One of the earliest SIMD computers is ILLIAC-IV (Barnes et al, 1968), which has been followed by a number of similar systems. The ILLIAC-IV was constructed by the Burroughs Corporation based on designs initiated at Westinghouse Electric and developed at the University of Illinois. It contained 64 processing elements arranged as an 8-by-8 array with every PE connected in a nearest neighbor mesh with end-around connection. Each processing element had a 2K memory module of 64-bit words.

The ICL DAP (Distributed Array Processor) contains 64-by-64 (i.e. 4096) processing elements and it has been used in both numeric and nonnumeric work including LSI design automation (Hunt, 1984) and sorting (Flanders & Reddaway, 1984).

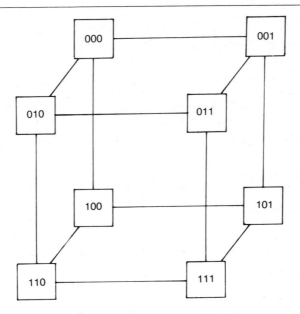

Fig. 2.16(a)   A 3-cube network

The MPP (massively parallel processor) is another example of an SIMD machine. It was built in the late 1970s by Goodyear Aerospace for use at NASA earth stations. It contains 128-by-128 processing elements thus capable of performing 16,384 single bit instructions simultaneously.

The Connection Machine was built by Thinking Machines Corporation (TMC) of Massachusetts, U.S.A. (Frenkel, 1986). It is based on a cube interconnection network and can provide massive parallelism by accommodating up to 65,536 PEs. Processors can be dynamically linked in The Connection Machine which allows reconfiguration to cater for the natural data structure of a problem.

2.4.3   Multiple instruction, multiple data stream (MIMD)

A *MIMD* system typically consists of a number of processors each capable of executing its own program on data obtained from a dedicated memory module. There are various designs within this category, with a major distinguishing feature being the interconnection network.

C.mmp, Cm*, HEP and PACS-32
Among the significant MIMD projects are Carnegie–Mellon University's C.mmp and Cm*. C.mmp consists of 16 processors and 16 storage modules connected by a cross-bar switch matrix (see Figure 2.9). A processor can

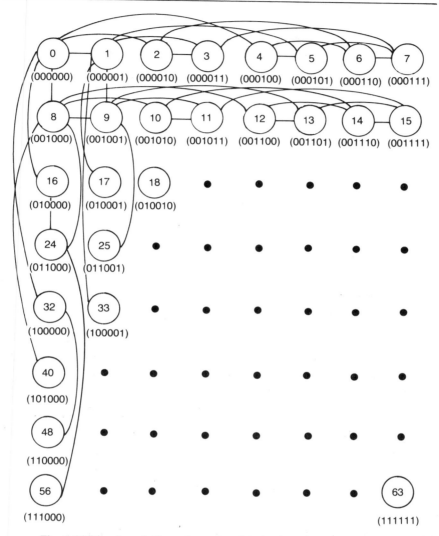

Fig. 2.16(b) A partial two-dimensional projection of a binary 6-cube

have access to any storage module. However, the complexity of this switching mechanism restricts the number of processors and storage modules that can be used practically.

A different design approach, a hierarchical model, was used in Cm*. The basic node is a (processor, local memory) pair called a computer module or Cm. Several Cms are connected via a bus to form a cluster, while clusters are connected via an intercluster bus. This arrangement can support a large number of processors. The Cm* implementation consists of 50 LSI-11 microprocessors.

The Heterogeneous Element Processor (HEP) of Denelcor, Inc. is claimed to be the first commercially available MIMD system (Hwang and Briggs, 1984). It contains up to 16 process execution modules (PEM) and up to 128 data memory modules (DMM). The interconnection system is a high speed, packet switched network consisting of an arbitrary number of nodes. Each node has three ports for input and output of packets to and from its neighbors. The neighbors may be PEMs, DMMs, subsystems or other nodes. However, it seems that the market was not quite ready for HEP and so Denelcor, Inc. declared itself bankrupt in 1985 after selling six $7 million HEP machines over a period of about five years (Frenkel, 1986).

The nearest neighbor mesh with end-around connection is the design used in the PACS-32 supercomputer (Hoshino et al, 1983) built at the University of Tsukuba as a synchronizable MIMD processor array with 32 PEs. Constructed for a range of scientific calculations, it has been used in the areas of nuclear reactor calculation, aerodynamics and molecular dynamics modeling in solid state physics.

The Cosmic Cube and the T Series from FPS

The Cosmic Cube is an experimental parallel computer designed and built in the early 1980s at the California Institute of Technology (Seitz, 1985). At the time of Seitz's report, the machine consisted of 64 small computers working in an MIMD mode. The individual computers, called nodes, are interconnected in a six dimensional hypercube also called a binary 6-cube (see Figure 2.16). Each node is connected through bidirectional, asynchronous communication channels to six other nodes.

Message passing, instead of shared variables, is the chosen interprocess communication scheme. Processes execute concurrently at any node under the control of an OS kernel which, among other things, handles the queuing and routing of messages. Application programs in high energy physics, astrophysics, fluid mechanics, seismology and other large and demanding computations in science and engineering can be developed on the Cosmic Cube. Of major significance is the basis that this project has laid for the development of supercomputers with thousands of nodes. One of these supercomputers is The Connection Machine discussed earlier.

Another example is the T Series from FPS. The T Series is a series of parallel machines built by Floating Point Systems, Inc. (FPS) of Oregon, U.S.A. (Frenkel, 1986). It is felt that, based as it is on the well-tested Cosmic Cube, the T Series should do well on the commercial market. It is expected to perform well in large-scale simulation, wave equations and the heavily floating point VLSI applications. The highest configuration of the T Series contains 16,384 PEs.

2.4.4　SIMD/MIMD

Some parallel processing projects have been undertaken to operate in both SIMD and MIMD modes. Purdue University's PASM is such a project. They envisaged a dynamically reconfigurable multiprocessor system with over a thousand PEs. The fundamental design approach and a 30-processor prototype are described by Siegal et al (1984).

Briefly, PASM is a partitionable SIMD/MIMD machine aimed at exploiting the parallelism in image processing, pattern recognition, speech understanding and biomedical signal processing. The dynamic reconfiguration facility offers the opportunity to execute an algorithm in either the SIMD or MIMD mode depending on which is more efficient. It also allows the same set of PEs to be used by a task requiring algorithms that employ both modes.

2.4.5　Systolic arrays

A multiprocessor system can be designed to execute a specific algorithm. The number of processors used and the interconnection of these processors will be determined by the algorithm. A systolic array – a collection of synchronized simple PEs designed for a particular algorithm – (Kung, 1984) fits into this category.

The name 'systolic' refers to the following design principle. Data enter at the perimeter of the array, then step through the array via the neighboring PEs. Each PE can accept input from two or three neighbors, perform a simple operation and send output to its neighbors.

Some problems that have been addressed by systolic units include very high speed multiplications (Hurson and Shirazi, 1985) and matrix computations (Chuang and He, 1985).

Since the systolic algorithm may be required in a range of computational tasks, systolic arrays are implemented as special purpose functional units within a general purpose computer.

2.5　NON VON NEUMANN-TYPE COMPUTERS

The traditional von Neumann architecture has dominated computer design. It is a sequential system involving the following steps: an instruction is fetched from memory, it is interpreted then the relevant data items are fetched from memory; the instruction is executed, after which the program counter is incremented to point to the next instruction in the sequence.

Data-flow and *reduction* machines represent a fundamental departure from this tradition (Dennis, 1979; Treleaven et al, 1982).

2.5.1 Data-flow machines

As the name 'data-flow' suggests, such machines are designed to allow the data elements to flow through a collection of processors, with inputs to each processor appropriately modified through some computation and the output results relayed to other processors. Sequencing is therefore not enforced by the architecture. Computations can be performed in parallel with the only sequencing being that which is determined by the character-istics of the problem.

A data-flow graph can be constructed to model the solution path. In the graph, the nodes depict the processors at which the operations are per-formed and the directed arcs indicate the paths along which the data flow. A node executes when it has received all its input items. On completing the operation, it puts the result onto its output arcs and may then indicate its readiness to accept new input. The arrival of data invokes the computa-tion hence it is called a *data-driven* system.

Figure 2.17 shows a data-flow graph for the problem

$$A = (B + C) * (D - E).$$

A data-flow machine contains several PEs each capable of executing a small instruction set. Each PE has a number of input and output arcs. Data are relayed along the arcs in tokens (a formatted bit frame) in a packet communication scheme (see Figure 2.18). Details on communication schemes are given in Chapter 3.

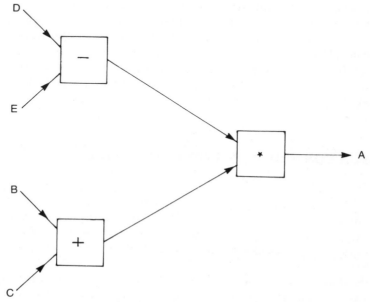

Fig. 2.17 A data-flow graph of A = (B + C) * (D − E)

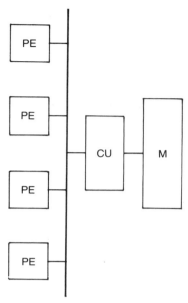

Fig. 2.18   A simple data-flow machine with the PEs connected to a bus

There is a memory section for holding the operations and operands. Instructions are selected from the memory and directed to the appropriate PEs. When packets arrive on the input arcs, the PE executes and puts out the result onto its output arcs. A mechanism is used to control the flow of input tokens.

One method is to let the PEs send acknowledgement tokens back up the input arcs. This feedback system indicates that the PE is ready for more input. Another method involves designing the arcs as first in, first out queues thus providing buffer space for tokens. Figure 2.18 shows a simple machine design.

Treleaven et al (1982) have described in some detail some of the significant data-flow computer projects. They used implementations at MIT, Manchester and elsewhere to demonstrate the different ways in which a data-flow machine can be constructed.

The MIT data-flow computer
The MIT data-flow computer consists of five major units:

(a) the memory section;
(b) the processing section;
(c) the arbitration network;
(d) the control network; and
(e) the distribution network.

The memory section holds the instructions and the destination addresses for the results. These instructions are enabled when data operands have arrived and the output arcs for the results are free. The data operands are sent by the distribution network while the control network sends control packets to indicate that output arcs are free.

Enabled instructions with their operands are sent via the arbitration network to respective specialist processing elements in the processing section. After the instructions are executed in the processing section, the results are sent in data packets and control packets to the memory section. The data packets travel through the distribution network to become operands for other instructions, while the control packets go via the control network to indicate to these instructions that they can be enabled.

The Manchester data-flow computer
The Manchester data-flow computer also contains five major units:

(a) the switch;
(b) the token queue;
(c) the matching store;
(d) the instruction store; and
(e) the processing unit.

Each instruction operates on one or two input data tokens and outputs either one or two data tokens. Tokens enter the computer through the switch and join the token queue. Since an instruction can operate on one or two tokens, a token can be one of a pair or a single input. If it is one of a pair the token goes to the matching store on leaving the queue where either a match is found and the pair moves on to the instruction store, or it awaits the arrival of a match. If the token is a single input, it bypasses the matching store and goes directly to the instruction store.

The input token(s) and the respective instruction are combined in the instruction store and then routed to the processing unit where any free processor from among its set of identical processors is selected to execute the instruction. Result tokens may, via the switch, leave the system or reenter the token queue.

CEDAR
The data-flow model is not restricted to instruction level distribution. The individual nodes could be designed to execute procedures. Gajski et al (1984) of the University of Illinois at Urbana Champaign outlined a large scale multiprocessor project called CEDAR, which would provide general purpose computing capabilities and operate in macro data-flow mode. There is the notion of a compound function – loosely described as a chunk of program – which will be the nodes in the data-flow graph.

2.5.2 Reduction machines

Reduction machines represent another line of departure from von Neumann-type architecture. In a reduction computer, an instruction is a function which, when evaluated, replaces the reference to the function by the present value of the function. Every occurrence of a symbol is viewed as a function reference. Therefore, the reference to a symbol demands that an operation be performed to replace that symbol by its value. The machine can therefore be classified as *demand-driven*. Each symbol should have a unique definition within a program.

For example, let us assume that the value of A must be computed for

$$A = (B + C)*(D - E).$$

This definition of A can be rewritten as the following sequence of definitions or functions.

$$A = F*G$$
$$F = B + C; G = D - E$$
$$B = 1; C = 3; D = 4; E = 2$$

The reduction machine will progressively reduce the referenced symbol, A, to its value by following the nested definitions. The evaluation can therefore take the following pattern:

Step 1: the reference 'A' demands its replacement by 'F * G';
Step 2: the references to 'F' and 'G' demand their replacement by 'B + C' and 'D − E' respectively, giving (B + C)*(D − E);
Step 3: the inner + and − operators demand replacements for 'B', 'C', 'D' and 'E' giving ((1 + 3)*(4 − 2));
Step 4: (1 + 3) and (4 − 2) are reduced to 4 and 2 respectively;
Step 5: (4*2) is reduced to 8.

The number of operations that can be done in parallel is significant. This parallelism can be exploited by allocating the reduction of the sub-expressions to different PEs. For example, at Step 2, one PE can operate on F while another PE can operate on G.

Different approaches have been taken in the implementation of reduction computers. Figure 2.19 shows a hierarchical organization of PEs accessing a common memory of definitions. Control measures must be employed to ensure that not more than one PE is working on the same subexpression at the same time. A communication scheme has to be established to permit the distribution of subexpressions, the transmission of definitions and the relaying of results.

In Chapter 7 we will look at some parallel language projects which involve reduction machines. Among those discussed will be the FP language which is the machine language used by the North Carolina cellular tree machine; LISP, a dialect of which forms the basis of the

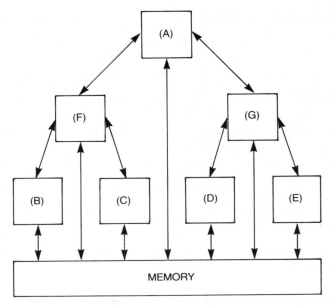

Fig. 2.19 A simple reduction machine showing the computation of
$$A = (B + C) * (D - E)$$

machine language for the Utah Applicative Multiprocessing System (AMPS); and an implementation technique developed by D.A. Turner (1979) which forms the basis for the design of Cambridge University's SKIM reduction machine (Treleaven et al, 1982). Let us look briefly at the Newcastle reduction machine.

The Newcastle reduction machine
The Newcastle reduction machine (Treleaven et al, 1982) has three major components:

(a) a common memory unit;
(b) a set of identical, asynchronous processing units; and
(c) a segmented *shift register*.

The expression being evaluated is in the shift register from which the processing units obtain subexpressions for reduction. The definitions required for the reduction process are obtained from the common memory unit, to which each processing unit has direct access. One of the major uses of this computer is the testing of different reduction language schemes.

Each processing unit has four registers which contain information relevant to the actions that must be performed on the subexpression that was obtained from the shift register. Starvation and deadlock problems can arise from the asynchronous operation of the processing units. Therefore certain protocols have been established to regulate accesses to the shift register.

2.6 SUMMARY

Many computational tasks can be divided into subtasks which need not be executed sequentially. Multiprocessors, multicomputers and computer networks provide opportunities for the distribution of computation and, therefore, for exploiting inherent parallelism.

One of the major motivations for developing such systems is the need for greater processing speeds. Pipeline processors, which permit the start of an instruction before the completion of previous instructions, have met some of this demand for faster processing. However, the computation may possess a certain distribution property that is not exploited by the pipeline processor.

A hierarchical network of computers can be used where the job can be divided into a hierarchy of procedures or programs, each of which can be executed at a different site. Processors in a multicomputer system or in a client-server network model can be dedicated to perform specific functions, e.g. file management, text handling, floating-point computations, and their services can be requested when these functions are needed. Furthermore, processors may cooperate on the running of any type of job selected from a single queue of jobs. One of the major concerns here is to ensure efficient scheduling of tasks among these processors.

Multiprocessor systems share a global memory and are managed by a single operating system. Distribution of computation can take place at a process level to support which there must be adequate interprocessor synchronization and communication mechanisms.

Recent developments in parallel architecture, made possible largely through considerable strides in VLSI technology, permit parallel processing at the single instruction level. Among the parallel projects are massively parallel systems consisting of thousands of processing elements.

These parallel machines can be divided into a number of categories. These include:

(a) *associative processors* which allow parallel searching of memory using the content of a word as the argument;
(b) *single instruction, multiple data stream* (SIMD) computers, which perform the same operation on many data items simultaneously;
(c) multiple instruction, multiple data stream (MIMD) computers, which perform different instructions on many data operands simultaneously;

(d) computers allowing both SIMD and MIMD modes of operation; and

(e) **systolic arrays** which are made up of a collection of simple PEs designed for a particular algorithm.

Significant developments are also seen in the area of non von Neumann computers. Two main streams of activity are:

(a) *data-flow machines* in which the PEs execute as soon as they receive data; and

(b) *reduction machines* which replace function references by their definitions.

2.7 QUESTIONS

2.1 What are some of the reasons for building computer systems to facilitate distributed and parallel computing?

2.2 Indicate some ways in which a computational task can be distributed.

2.3 How does a pipeline vector processor differ from an array processor?

2.4 Distinguish among the following systems:

(a) multiprocessor systems;

(b) multicomputer systems; and

(c) computer networks.

2.5 What job scheduling schemes can be used in a multicomputer system?

2.6 Why are synchronization and communication important in a multiprocessor system? Indicate ways in which these issues can be handled.

2.7 What similarity is there between an associative processor and an SIMD computer?

2.8 Suggest applications that are most suitable for each of the following systems:

(a) vector processor;

(b) array processor;

(c) MIMD computer; and

(d) systolic array.

2.9 Briefly define the following:

(a) data-flow machine;

(b) reduction machine.

2.10 Compare and contrast data-flow and reduction machines.

2.11 (a) Draw a data-flow graph to evaluate the function

$$f(x) = (b + c)x - d/e.$$

(b) Use a reduction scheme to compute $f(x)$ as defined in (a).

2.12 Explain how the following computation can be handled on an MIMD machine:

$$C(i, j) = S * A(i, j) + (B(i, j))/(T(i) - j) \text{ for } i, j = 1, \ldots 10000.$$

2.8 REFERENCES

1 Barnes, G.H. et al, 1968. 'The ILLIAC-IV Computer', *IEEE Transactions on Computers* C-17, 746–757.

2 Chuang, H.Y.H. and He Guo, 1985. 'A versatile systolic array for matrix computations', *The 12th Annual International Symposium on Computer Architecture*, 315–322.

3 Deitel, H.M., 1984. *An Introduction to Operating Systems*, Reading, Ma, Addison-Wesley Pub. Co.

4 Dennis, J.B., 1979. 'The varieties of data flow computers', *Proceedings of the First International Conference on Distributed Computing Systems*, 430–439.

5 Enslow, P.H., 1977. 'Multiprocessor Organization', *ACM Computing Surveys*, **9**, 1(Mar), 103–129.

6 Flanders, P.M. and Reddaway, S.F., 1984. 'Sorting on DAP', *ICL Technical Journal*, **4**, 2(Nov), 139–145.

7 Flynn, M.J., 1966. 'Very high-speed computing systems', *Proceedings of IEEE*, **54**, 1901–1909.

8 Frenkel, K.A., 1986. 'Evaluating two massively parallel machines', *Communications of the ACM*, **29**, 8, 752–758.

9 Gajski, D. et al, 1984. 'CEDAR: A large scale multiprocessor', *ACM Computer Architecture News*, **11**, 1, 7–11.

10 Garside, R.G., 1980. *The Architecture of Digital Computers*, New York, Oxford University Press.

11 Gorsline, G.W., 1986. *Computer Organization, Hardware/Software* (2nd edition), Englewood Cliffs: Prentice Hall Inc.

12 Hoshino, T. et al, 1983. 'PACS: A parallel microprocessor array for scientific calculations', *ACM Transactions on Computer Systems*, **1**, 3, 195–221.

13 Hunt, D.J., 1984. 'Tracking of LSI chips and printed circuit boards using the ICL Distributed Array Processor', *ICL Technical Journal*, **4**, 2(Nov), 131–138.

14 Hurson, A.R. and Shirazi, B., 1985. 'A systolic multiplier unit and its VLSI design', *The 12th Annual International Symposium on Computer Architecture*, 302–309. Boston, Ma.

15 Hwang, K. and Briggs, F.A., 1984. *Computer Architecture and Parallel Processing*, New York: McGraw-Hill.

16 Kung, H.T., 1984. 'Systolic Algorithms', in *Large Scale Scientific Computation* (pp. 127–139) edited by S.V. Parter, Orlando, Fa: Academic Press, Inc.

17 Peterson, J. and Silberschatz, A., 1983. *Operating System Concepts*, Reading: Ma., Addison-Wesley.

18 Seitz, C.L., 1985. The Cosmic Cube, *Communications of the ACM*, **28**, 1(Jan), 22–33.

19 Siegal, H.J., et al, 1984. 'PASM: A reconfigurable parallel system for image processing', *ACM Computer Architecture News*, **12**, 4, 7–19.

20 Tanenbaum, A.S., 1981. *Computer Networks*, Englewood Cliffs: Prentice Hall Inc.

21 Treleaven, P.C., Brownbridge, D.R. and Hopkins, R.P., 1982. 'Data-driven and demand-driven computer architecture', *ACM Computing Surveys*, **14**, 1, 93–143.

22 Turner, D.A., 1979. 'A New Implementation Technique for Applicative Languages', *Software – Practice and Experience*, **9**, 31–49.

CHAPTER THREE

COMMUNICATIONS AND COMPUTER NETWORKS

Computer networks have increased the opportunities for man-to-man communication. It is necessary to look at some of the basic principles of communication in order to appreciate the many alternative techniques available and to understand how constraints of one kind or another can affect the design decisions. The following sections introduce aspects of information theory relevant to computer networks, show how the layered architecture builds on that theoretical base and examine the different topological forms that the networks can assume.

3.1 COMMUNICATIONS

Man-to-man communication is as old as man himself. However this communication has undergone significant change with important high-points being the transmission of information by wire, and the use of radio and satellite techniques. These achievements were made possible through the discovery and formulation of certain basic principles which prescribe the capabilities and the inevitable constraints.

3.1.1 Some theory

In order to communicate, a sound or signal must be sent and subsequently received and understood. Therefore, we need a *transmitter* (to send), a *medium* (to convey), and a *receiver*. In face-to-face oral communication, we do not stop to think of the basic principles involved, but they are there nonetheless.

The sound travels in *waves* (vibrations) through the air, which repeat themselves as they go, i.e. the waves are **periodic**. The loudness or strength of

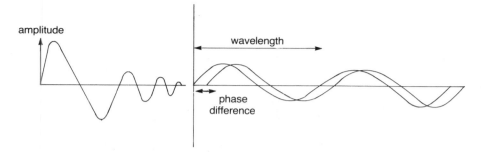

Fig. 3.1 Analog waveforms indicating amplitude, wavelength and phase

the sound determines the *amplitude* and the pitch (whether high or low) determines the *frequency* which is expressed in cycles (complete waveforms) per second or *Hertz (Hz)* (see Figure 3.1). As distance increases, the sound wave weakens and, due to other interferences, it may even change its form rendering accurate reception impossible. This problem is called *attenuation*.

To extend the distance covered, electrical signals can be passed along a wire. This requires a suitable transmitting device to convert the sound into the signal, and a suitable receiver to do the reverse. Mapping of the sound wave onto the signal is accomplished by varying the electrical current and voltage levels in the wire.

Speech signals vary continuously over time and are therefore in the category of waves which are referred to as *analog waves*. These differ from the *digital signaling* of electronic computers. Binary coded forms are used in most computers today and the representation of a string of binary digits (bits) in computer communications approximates a square wave (see Figure 3.2). In order to transmit such a signal, two values of voltage are used: one value to indicate the 'zero' bit, and the other to denote the 'one' bit. The frequency in this case is determined by the number of times the signal changes in one second. This is usually referred to as the *baud rate*. If each signal change represents one bit, then the maximum *transmission rate* of bits is equal to the baud rate.

The change of signal may represent other digits. For example, four distinct voltages could be used, each associated with one of the digits: 0, 1,

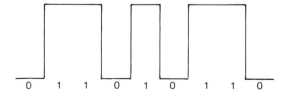

Fig. 3.2 An example of a binary signal

2 and 3, i.e. the binary values 00, 01, 10 and 11; or eight signal changes could be used to distinguish among the octal digits 0, 1, 2, 3, 4, 5, 6 and 7; and so on.

If it is assumed that the signal changes once every millisecond (msec), then, where two distinct voltages are used, i.e. each signal change represents a bit, the information rate is 1000 bits/sec (bps) – the same as the baud rate. Where each signal is one of four values then two bits of information are conveyed in each msec therefore generating an information rate of 2000 bps – twice the baud rate. In the octal case, the information rate is 3000 bps.

The range of frequencies that a physical medium can transmit is limited. Sometimes this limit is artificially created. It is called the **bandwidth** of the channel. From Fourier analysis it is understood that, a square wave (like other periodic waves) can be expressed as the sum of an infinite number of **sinusoidal waves** with increasing frequencies and decreasing amplitudes. The inability of the medium to transmit these higher frequency components can seriously distort the signal (see Figure 3.3). The higher the frequency of the square wave the more serious will be the distortion.

This limit of the medium to transmit data has been expressed in two fundamental theorems in communications. One is *Nyquist's theorem* which states that if W is the bandwidth of the channel and V is the number of discrete signal values then

$$\text{maximum data rate} = 2W \log_2 V \text{ bps.}$$

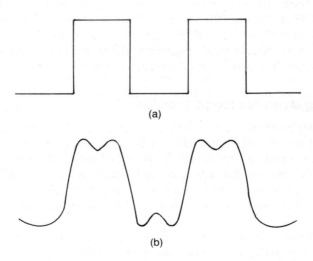

(a)

(b)

Fig. 3.3   An indication of the distortion (b) introduced by transmitting a square wave (a) using an insufficient number of Fourier components

Binary digits have two discrete signal values, therefore in this case the maximum data rate equals 2W bps.

However, the problem of noise must be considered. This could be viewed as the inherent physical property of the medium to generate random noise. This noise factor is considered in the equation of *Shannon* which states that

$$\text{maximum number of bits/sec} = W \log_2 (1 + S/N)$$

where S/N is the signal to noise ratio. This indicates that there are further limits to the amount of information that can be conveyed by the channel and defines the *channel capacity*.

The noise is expressed in units called *decibels (dB)*. The relationship between the decibel value and the ratio S/N is

$$\text{decibel value} = 10 \log_{10} S/N.$$

From Nyquist's theorem it follows that the maximum data rate can be increased by increasing V – the number of signal values. However, any increase in V must be limited by Shannon's equation. In particular, the following relation must hold:

$$2 \log_2 V < \log_2 (1 + S/N).$$

Some typical dB values quoted for the telephone system are 20 dB and 30 dB. These generate S/N ratios of 100 and 1000 respectively. An S/N value of 100 results in a maximum integral value for V of 8; while an S/N value of 1000 returns a maximum integral value for V of about 32. With 3000 Hz bandwidth telephone lines, these values of V would produce maxima of 18,000 bps and 30,000 bps respectively. However, these rates are difficult to achieve in practice using the voice-grade telephone system. Furthermore, if a significantly high bandwidth channel is available then these noise levels may not constitute a serious restriction.

3.1.2 Digital-to-analog conversion

A wide telephone network is available for speech communications. As mentioned earlier, these speech signals are analog and the telephone network was designed to handle these waves with a frequency range of 300 Hz to 3300 Hz which is adequate for the human voice. Installing a new network to transmit digital signals over long distances is prohibitively expensive, therefore in many instances the existing telephone lines are used.

Modulation techniques are employed to allow the digital signal to be carried on the analog channel. A device is needed to convert the signal from digital to analog at the sending end and to convert from analog to digital at the receiving end. This device is called a *modem (modulator/*

demodulator). Three modulation techniques used are *frequency shift keying, phase modulation* and *amplitude modulation*

Frequency shift keying (FSK)

In FSK, the digital signal is coded in frequencies. Each discrete signal value or voltage is converted to a different frequency. Demodulation involves the opposite operation. For the binary signal only two frequency values are needed (see Figure 3.4). One constraint is that, in order to detect

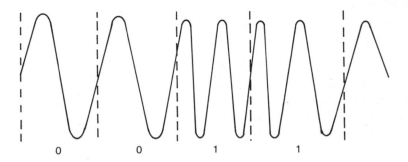

Fig. 3.4   Frequency modulation or frequency shift keying

the frequency, at least half a cycle must be transmitted. Therefore the time interval, I secs, between the changes in the value of the signal must be greater than the time to complete half of the cycle, i.e. half the period, T, of the wave.

Since the lowest frequency used has the longest period, then

$$I > (1/2)T$$

where T is the period of the lowest frequency, f, that is output by the modulator. This I will be large enough to accommodate the shorter cycles of the higher frequencies. Since the number of signal changes per second gives the baud rate, b, then

$$b = 1/I$$

i.e. $1/b > (1/2)(1/f)$, therefore:

$$f > (1/2)b.$$

Hence the lowest frequency used must be greater than half of the baud rate of the data signal.

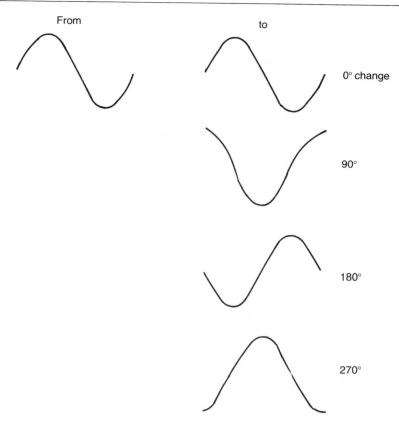

Fig. 3.5 Differential phase modulation

Phase modulation (PM)

In PM, the signal is coded in *phase changes*. In a phase change the wave retains its shape but there is a shift in its position (see Figure 3.1). Therefore the same frequency is used, but, by dedicating distinct phase changes to particular digital values, the signal can be transmitted.

Large phase changes are used to facilitate detection. At the start of the signaling interval there is a test to determine the extent of change relative to the state in the previous interval. *Differential phase modulation* allows four possible phase changes: 0, 90, 180 and 270 degrees (see Figure 3.5). With four such changes, four distinct values can be coded. Therefore two bits of information are transmitted in each phase change.

Amplitude modulation (AM)

In AM the digital values are coded as specific changes in amplitude (see Figure 3.6). The same frequency is used, but by altering the amplitude, distinct signals can be conveyed. This technique is usually combined with PM to increase the number of combinations that could be represented by the signal change. For example, if each sampling interval can have any one of four phase changes plus any one of two amplitude changes then eight different digits or three bits of information can be transmitted per interval, i.e. each signal change represents an octal digit.

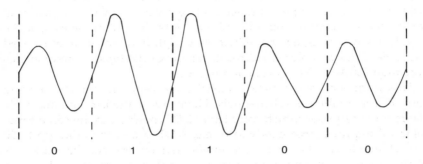

Fig. 3.6   Amplitude modulation

Advantages in no modulation
There are limitations on transmission capacity in using the analog telephone system. There are many advantages in using a network that can transmit the digital signals. Errors can be monitored more easily, digital processors can be used for aspects of circuit management, and multiplexing techniques are available to permit more efficient use of the network. Therefore, in spite of the great cost, many telephone authorities are changing from the analog system to digital. The analog signals can be converted to digital thus opening up vast opportunities for both voice and computer communications.

3.1.3   Transmission media

Some of the media used in communications are twisted pair, coaxial cable, optical fibers, radio frequencies and communications satellites (U.K. Post Office, 1975; Gee, 1983). A brief introduction to these media follows.

Twisted pair
A pair of wires is twisted in the form of a helix and one or more of these pairs will be enclosed in a single outer sheath. It is generally used for analog transmissions, but it has been used in digital signaling. It is often the cheapest form of communications media available.

It is still used in many telephone systems and most often accommodates a maximum data rate of 9.6 kbps. It is susceptible to a great deal of electrical interference which results in high error rates. Furthermore, due to relatively high emissions, it can be easily tapped, which reduces its suitability in areas where security is of major concern.

Coaxial cable
Instead of a pair of wires to conduct the electrical signals, the coaxial cable has a solid central copper conductor surrounded by insulating material over which is a conducting tube with an outer insulating layer. Coaxial cable has a lower degree of attenuation at high frequencies than twisted pair cable. Coaxial cable provides data rates over 10 *Mbps* and frequencies more than 300 *MHz* (M = mega or million).

This frequency range makes coaxial cable very suitable for carrying many lower frequency subchannels. Hence its popularity among cable television enterprises which offer tens of TV channels at the same time. Color TV requires large bandwidth, e.g. 6 MHz, and therefore up to 50 such channels can be easily accommodated on the coaxial cable. Its relatively low error rate, large capacity and the flexibility it allows in implementation have made it a popular choice for LANs.

Optical fibers
These transmit light rather than electrical signals, which means that this medium is unaffected by electrical interference. There is a central filament surrounded by a layer of material which prevents the rays of light from reflecting outwards, thus increasing the transmission capability along the length of the filament. It is necessary to convert the electrical signals to light pulses before transmission and perform the opposite operation at the destination point. This conversion introduces additional cost and complexity in design. However, the high quality and rates (over 1 billion Hz (GHz)) that can be achieved even in areas of disturbing levels of electrical interference make optical fibers an attractive option. Error rates for optical fibers have been quoted as low as one bit in one billion bits.

Radio frequencies
Messages are broadcast using dedicated channels from the radio frequency band. In using ground-based radio transmission, a few hundred kilometers can be covered. ALOHA pioneered the use of this technique in computer communications. It is the first computer network to be developed around broadcast radio techniques. It was built by a team at the University of Hawaii to link computing facilities on the Hawaiian islands. This network became operational in the early 1970s and the transmission techniques employed have contributed to the development of broadcast transmission methods. These methods address the problems

involving noise and channel allocation which arise in the use of radio frequencies.

Satellite
Communication satellites can be used for computer communications over long distances. These satellites can be viewed as large repeating stations which receive the upwardly directed signal and rebroadcast the amplified signal to locations on the earth. These locations may occupy an area ranging from a few hundred kilometers to a major portion of the earth's surface. The propagation time (the time taken for the first bit of information to complete the round trip from the ground to the satellite and back) via satellite is close to 300 msec.

However there is a threshold in the length of the message beyond which the total delay is shorter than via the commonly used terrestrial links. This is due to the faster bit rates (up to 50 Mbps) provided by satellite transmissions. For example, at 50 Mbps the total time to transmit 50 million bits is 1 sec + propagation time, i.e. 1.3 secs. With a terrestrial link that has a considerably lower bit rate, say 9.6 kbps, and a negligible propagation time, the amount of bits transmitted in 1.3 secs is about 12,000. Another useful factor in satellite communications is the fact that the cost of sending messages does not depend on the distance.

3.2 COMPUTER NETWORK ARCHITECTURE

A computer network is built upon a communications base, aspects of which have just been discussed. In order to facilitate the design, construction and maintenance of these networks, a layered architecture has been used in network design. For each layer there are the protocols which constitute a framework for the communication at that layer (see Chapter 1). However, because of the independent development of layered architectures, they tend to vary across networks. However the *International Standards Organization (ISO)* has proposed a standard architecture in order to facilitate the interconnection of different networks. It is a seven layer model called the reference model of *Open Systems Interconnection (OSI)* (see Figure 3.7).

These seven layers range from the hardware dependent layer at the bottom of the hierarchy to the user applications environment at the top. They include, beginning at the lowest layer:

(a) The *physical layer* which is responsible for the transmission of the raw bits over the communication channel;
(b) The *data link layer* which transforms the raw bit stream into a string of bits which is free of transmission errors;
(c) The *network layer* which handles the routing within the subnet and determines the interface between the host and IMP;

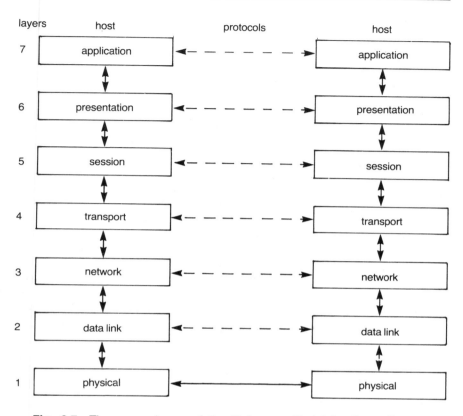

Fig. 3.7 The seven layers of the Reference Model for Open Systems Interconnection (OSI)

(d) The ***transport layer*** which is responsible for the safe transfer of messages from one application process at a host to another;

(e) The ***session layer*** which is the layer in which connection is initiated for a communication exercise;

(f) The ***presentation layer*** which resolves differences in formats among the various hosts; and

(g) The ***application layer*** where the functions or applications that the user can run are created.

ARPANET of the US Department of Defense, IBM's ***SNA*** and Digital's DECnet ***DNA*** all vary in different areas from the reference model for Open System's Interconnection (Tanenbaum, 1981).

The Advanced Research Projects Agency of the U.S. Department of Defense started developing ARPANET as a computer network research project in the late 1960s. It became operational in 1969 as an experimental system and it now links scores of computers throughout North America and across the ocean to the UK and Western Europe. The ARPANET project has contributed immensely to computer network development. It is one of the best known examples of a wide area network and many of the terms used in the literature on networks have their origin in ARPANET.

IBM's SNA – Systems Network Architecture – has the following seven layers:

7	End user	user applications
6	NAU service	network addressable unit layer – session services, text compression, code conversion, etc
5	Data flow control	session management
4	Transmission control	arrangement of host-to-host connection
3	Path control	network control: routing, flow control, etc.
2	Data link control	error control for bit streams; uses *SDLC* protocol – Synchronous Data Link Control
1	Physical	permits transmission of raw bits

Digital Equipment Corporation's DNA – Digital Network Architecture has the following eight layers (see Digital, 1985).

8	User	user applications
7	Network management	systems management
6	Network application	application support for layers 7 and 8, e.g. file transfer, remote file access
5	Session control	session management
4	End communication	connection management, data flow, end-to-end error control, etc.
3	Routing	network routing, congestion control
2	Data link	error control for bit streams
1	Physical link	permits transmission of raw bits

The ISO model will be discussed in some detail in the following subsections. Whereas the ISO is concerned with standards in general, another body, the *CCITT* (the abbreviation of the French name of the International Consultative Committee for Telegraphs and Telephones), are responsible for coordinating international telecommunications and making recommendations for international standards. Clearly, there is some overlap between these two organizations as the ISO's Reference Model deals with computer networks which involve aspects of tele-communications. Certain CCITT standards are directly applicable to the first three layers of the ISO model (Davies et al, 1979) and these will be referred to briefly at the appropriate points.

3.2.1   The physical layer

This is concerned with the transmission of strings of bits from one host to the other. It is, therefore, necessary to choose a suitable signaling tech-nique, transmission medium and related equipment to provide an acceptable communication channel. Other concerns would be whether or not to include *multiplexing* to provide better utilization of the available bandwidth, making the choice between *circuit switching* and *packet switching* techniques, the handling of terminals, and the management of errors.

3.2.1.1   Multiplexing

Rather than installing several narrow-bandwidth physical channels, one wide-bandwidth channel is usually multiplexed, i.e. it is shared among many users. In order to avoid collisions of messages from separate sources, efficient sharing techniques must be employed. Multiplexing techniques can be categorized as either *frequency division multiplexing* (FDM) or *time division multiplexing* (TDM).

Frequency division multiplexing (FDM)
In FDM, the frequency range of a wide bandwidth physical link is divided up into several narrower channels. These narrower bandwidth channels will be adequate to meet the transmission requirements of the users to which they are exclusively allocated. Between each of these usable frequency bands there is an unused band which serves to reduce inter-ference across the boundaries of the channels. Since these narrower channels are for the exclusive use of those to whom they are allocated, it follows that these frequencies will be wasted whenever the users have nothing to transmit.

Time division multiplexing (TDM)
In TDM, each user is allocated a time slot during which time that user has exclusive use of the entire bandwidth. In its pure round robin form, it

could result in inefficient use of the physical channel. The user can only transmit when his turn comes around and all users get a turn even if they have nothing to send. Therefore, while some users will be allocated time when they have nothing to transmit, other users with heavy transmission loads will have to be satisfied with short transmission bursts and long unnecessary waits.

However, some amount of intelligence could be built into the system in order to allocate time slots according to user demand. This would generate a more efficient distribution of time slots. This attempt to allocate time slots on demand is called *statistical time division multiplexing*.

Statistical time division multiplexing (STDM)

In STDM, time slots are not preassigned. If a station has something to transmit, it is given the channel. Furthermore, rather than having the number of time slots equal to the number of stations as in TDM, the number of stations will be more than the number of slots. The ratio of stations to time slots will be determined by expected traffic load, hence the reference to statistics. However this raises two issues:

(a) since any user can send at any time, a user cannot now be identified merely by the use of a dedicated time slot; and

(b) there can be more users ready to send than the number of time slots allocated.

Problem (a) can be solved by accommodating control and addressing information among the data relayed in the time slot. For example, the leading byte transmitted is adequate to carry a 1 bit control field and a 7 bit address.

The second issue can be dealt with by providing storage to queue the excess users or by disallowing their transmission attempts and forcing them to try again.

Although these constitute additional overhead on the *multiplexor*, experience has shown that the increase in channel utilization is significant enough to make the statistical multiplexor a viable option. Furthermore, the necessary intelligence can be readily implemented by using available microprocessor technology.

3.2.1.2 Circuit switching and packet switching

The existence of the physical communication link is necessary for the transmission of information whether it is via analog or digital signals. We have seen how the transmission capacity can be shared to permit multiple inputs onto one physical channel. However, there is another dimension to the use of these communication media which we will look at now.

In telephone conversation, there is usually a continuous interchange of information between the speakers, even if at times the responses may merely be grunts or chuckles. In order to accommodate this pattern, the convention is to give the caller and callee a complete end-to-end path for their exclusive use throughout the duration of the conversation. This technique is called *circuit switching*. The telephone system uses its switching equipment to establish this dedicated circuit.

Computer communications are essentially 'bursty' (varying amounts at irregular intervals), and sometimes there is no need for an immediate response. A dedicated circuit in a wide area computer network for long periods will therefore mean poor use of the communication resources.

Another approach is possible. When a user at a host has information to send, there is no attempt to dedicate an entire path before the transmission begins. Instead, the message is transferred to the first IMP (see Figure 1.4) where it is stored to be forwarded later, on an available link, to the next IMP. This hop-by-hop *store-and-forward* process takes place until the message reaches the destination host. This technique is referred to as *message switching*, where there is no limit on the length of the message *block* (Davies and Barber, 1973), which is determined by the amount of data the user has to transmit.

However, there are obvious difficulties in handling these variably sized blocks. Enough memory must be available at the intermediary IMPs, and short, important messages may have to wait behind long, unimportant ones. It is better to impose a fixed length on the block size. These fixed-length blocks are called *packets*, hence the name *packet switching*. A message is divided into a number of packets and each packet is handled independently of the other.

The division of the message into packets for independent transmission allows more messages to share the network at the same time. This can provide interactive information exchange, a benefit not easily available in the message switching scheme. There must be controls introduced to ensure accurate receipt of the message at the destination host.

Packet switching was put forward in the early 1960s by Paul Baran of the Rand Corporation, USA. At around the same time, Donald Davies of the UK National Physical Laboratory began the design of a computer network, NPL, using packet switching techniques. ARPANET also served as an important testing ground for packet switching. These pioneering projects demonstrated that packet switching was a suitable data transmission technique, and its use has become widespread in computer network design.

3.2.1.3 Terminal handling

At this level, there must exist the facility to handle the terminals connected to the host. These terminals are usually connected by a *multidrop* or *point-to-point* line to a terminal controller which is connected by one communication line to the computer (see Figure 3.8). The terminal controller uses a technique called *polling* to allow terminals which have information to transmit to begin transmitting. Each terminal is polled in

AUGUSTANA UNIVERSITY COLLEGE
LIBRARY

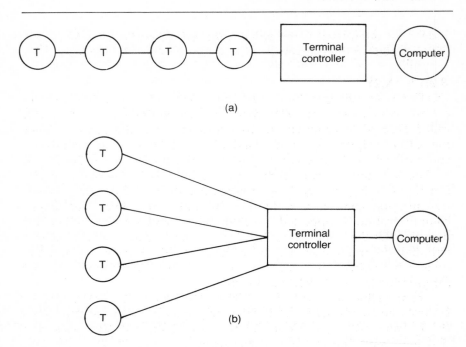

Fig. 3.8   (a) Multidrop line
(b) point-to-point line linking terminals to computer

turn. If the terminal has information to send, it does so only when it is polled. Multiplexing is used to share the line capacity of the common channel among the terminals.

3.2.1.4   Errors

One of the unpleasant facts of life in communications is that errors will occur, corrupting the data transmitted. These errors occur for a number of reasons including fluctuations in the background noise level of the channel and electromagnetic interference from neighboring electrical devices.

Methods must be employed to cope with these errors. Techniques used are based on the principle of adding extra bits to the data stream in order to form a code. This code is used by the receiver to determine the accuracy of the message block. There are two major categories into which these codes can be divided: *error correcting* and *error detecting*.

In error-correcting codes there must be enough redundant information so that the receiver can both determine that an error has occurred and what the correct value is. In error-detecting codes, the receiver merely detects that an error has occurred. The correct value cannot be reconstructed. The devices connected to the network should use the same procedure. The code most often used is the *polynomial code* or *cyclic redundancy code* (CRC) for which there are international standards (see section 3.2.2).

3.2.1.5 X.21

CCITT has specified standards pertaining to the communication between a host, which they call *DTE* (data terminal equipment), and its IMP called *DCE* (data communications equipment). At the physical layer, the CCITT digital signaling standard is called *X.21*. It defines the composition and function of the physical link between the DTE and DCE.

The X.21 link contains eight signaling lines each allocated a specific function (see Figure 3.9). These can be categorized as data transmission, transmission control, and information timing functions. *Full duplex* communication is supported, i.e. information can be transmitted in both directions at the same time. This differs from *half duplex* mode where, although information can be transmitted in both directions, it cannot be done in both directions at the same time; and from *simplex* mode in which information travels in only one direction.

Separate lines are used for the DTE-to-DCE and DCE-to-DTE data and control transmissions. The DTE sends data and control information along the T (Transmit) and C (Control) lines respectively. The DCE uses the R (Receive) and I (Indication) lines for the transmission of data and control information respectively. The C and I lines facilitate connection and disconnection operations. The other lines permit the timing and framing mechanisms necessary for character detection.

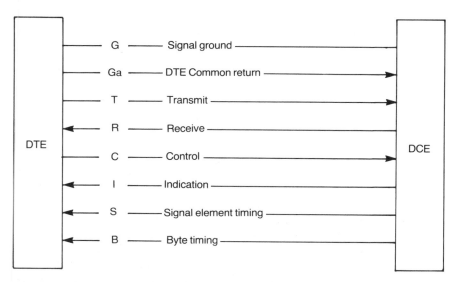

Fig. 3.9   The eight signaling lines of the X.21 link between DTE and DCE.
Andrew S. Tanenbaum, *Computer Networks*, © 1981, p. 109. Adapted by permission of Prentice Hall Inc., Englewood Cliffs, New Jersey

3.2.2   The data link layer

Link protocols are concerned with efficient and reliable transmission of information from one *node* (host or IMP) in the network to a neighboring node. In order for a host to communicate with another, the message will have to pass through the subnet, stopping at several IMPs along the way. Therefore it is essential that each node shoulders the responsibility of error-free transmission to a neighboring node. This layer addresses this link level responsibility which involves the IMP-to-IMP link as well as the host-to-IMP link.

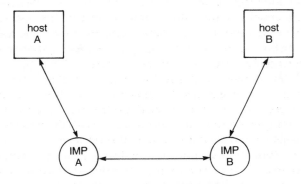

Fig. 3.10   IMP-to-IMP communication at the data link layer

Flag	Frame level control (FLC)	data	CRC (FCS)	Flag

Fig. 3.11   The format of a data link frame

For the purposes of this discussion, it can be assumed that host A has a message to send to host B. Host A is linked directly to IMP A, and host B is linked directly to IMP B. It is sufficient at this layer to imagine the existence of only one link in the subnet i.e. IMP A to IMP B (see Figure 3.10). The data link protocol that exists at the host-IMP link may differ from that at the IMP-IMP link. The following procedures are involved.

The data link layer at the host A uses the message block or packet received from the layer above to construct a *frame* which will be passed to the IMP A. This frame will then be transmitted to IMP B. If the subnet uses a different protocol then a different frame (containing the same message) will be constructed for the IMP-IMP transmission. The frame contains control information and the data message (see Figure 3.11).

A flag is used to indicate start and end of frame. This is a special bit pattern that cannot be used except for this purpose. However techniques are available which permit the same bit sequence to occur as a valid part of the message. One efficient technique is *bit stuffing*. For example, if the flag is 01111110, then no sequence of 6 '1' bits is allowed, a '0' bit is inserted (stuffed) after every sequence of five '1' bits.

The *frame level control (FLC)* includes kind of frame, sequence number and acknowledgment indication. The kind of frame field allows the distinction between control frames (i.e. no data being transmitted) and data frames. The sequence field is used to identify frames within some time interval. It is possible for a frame to be considered lost when in fact it has suffered an unusually long delay. It will then be retransmitted and therefore both the original and the duplicate can reach the receiver. The sequence number helps to solve this problem. Since in this case both frames will have the same sequence number, one will be rejected. The acknowledgment field indicates on return to the sender that an error-free frame has been received by the destination node.

The CRC (FCS) field contains the hardware computed cyclic redundancy code or *frame check sequence* (sometimes called *frame checksum*). On receipt of the frame, the data stream is used to compute the CRC. If the computed checksum does not agree with the one received, the frame is discarded and no acknowledgment is returned.

The CRC is a polynomial code obtained in the following manner. The bit string is treated as representative of a polynomial with each bit being a coefficient. If the string has n bits then the polynomial has the n terms, x^{n-1} to x^0. Therefore the string 10010011 represents the polynomial

$$1.x^7 + 0.x^6 + 0.x^5 + 1.x^4 + 0.x^3 + 0.x^2 + 1.x^1 + 1.x^0$$

i.e. $x^7 + x^4 + x^1 + 1$. To compute the FCS for the m-bit message, the corresponding m-term polynomial must be divided by some agreed *generator polynomial* using modulo-2 polynomial arithmetic. The remainder is the FCS and it is appended to the message.

These data link layer operations may seem simple, but in a realistic situation there will be varying numbers of unrelated message blocks arriving from different hosts thus making heavy demands on buffering and other management capabilities at the IMP.

X.25

The CCITT standard for this layer is called *X.25*, and it is a specification for the link between the DTE (host) and the DCE (IMP). It is based on the ISO link control protocol, *HDLC* (high-level data link control). It is a bit-oriented protocol, i.e. the content of the frame is regarded as an arbitrary string of bits, not an integral number of characters. Each frame begins and ends with a special 8-bit code called the flag field which delimits the frame. That flag is in fact 01111110, hexademical '7E'.

There are three types of frames: information, supervisory and unnumbered frame. The type of frame is indicated in the control field, which also has a 3 bit allocation for sequence number and a 3 bit provision for acknowledgment indication. There is an 8 bit address field which can be used in a multidrop line arrangement. In the point-to-point link, the address is used to distinguish between commands and responses, i.e. the transmitter (DTE or DCE) uses a code when sending a command that differs from that when it sends a response.

The information frame contains the information from layer 3, while the supervisory and unnumbered frames are for control (Cole, 1981). These frames are used to perform the functions relating to error-free transfer of packets. Before a packet can be transmitted, link connection must be set up with the remote DCE. To terminate the communication session there is an explicit disconnection of the link.

Data transfer is done using a *Go-Back-N ARQ* (automatic repeat request) technique. Frames must be acknowledged in the same sequence as they were sent. Assume therefore that a node has sent frames 1, 2, 3 and 4. An acknowledgment (ack) has been received for sequence number 1. The receiver detected an error in 2 and sent a negative acknowledgment (nak) indicating rejection of that frame. Therefore the sender must go back to 2 and repeat the transmission of 2, 3, 4 and so on. Retransmissions are also performed if there is no response from the receiver within the time-out interval. Since acknowledgments follow the same sequence, if an ack is received for 4 before an ack for 3 the sender can assume that 3 has been received.

The *window size* is the maximum number of frames that can be sent before an acknowledgment is received. In X.25 the sequence number field is three bits long. Therefore, eight distinct sequence numbers – 0 to 7 – are used. However the window size is 7 so that duplicate frames will not be mistaken for new frames. For example if the window size were 8, and acknowledgments were outstanding on frames 0 to 7, which are buffered at the receiver. The sender can time-out and retransmit frame 0 while the acknowledgment for the initial frame 0 is on its way from the receiver. The receiver will now have advanced his window to receive a new frame 0 and therefore will accept the duplicate as the new frame.

The FCS in X.25 is a 16 bit field obtained by using the CCITT generating polynomial: $x^{16} + x^{12} + x^5 + 1$.

3.2.3   The network layer

The network layer is responsible for host-to-host communications. At this layer, the host receives a packet of information from the layer above it, adds its protocol header to the packet and uses layer 2 to transmit it to the IMP. At that IMP, the network layer selects a route to another IMP then uses layer 2 to handle the link transmission. This process is repeated across the network until the packet is delivered to the destination host.

The protocol header information will depend on the type of service, i.e. *virtual call* or *datagram* service.

Virtual call and datagram

In the virtual call environment, a virtual circuit is established before the message is transmitted. This means that a particular route is set up and will be used to transmit all the data packets, in the right sequence, relating to the particular communication exercise. In the datagram service, the network transmits each packet as a separate unit by using the best possible route available at the time. It means that packets may arrive out of order and it is the responsibility of the receiver to reassemble them into the right sequence.

In virtual call, the packet needs a destination address only for setting up the connection. Subsequent to this, a logical channel number which was assigned at set-up time is used. In datagram, each packet must carry the explicit destination address.

Routing, flow control

The subnet will most certainly have a number of possible physical paths between two hosts. Therefore there is the need to choose the best route to transmit packets. This means employing routing algorithms of which there are many alternative designs. This routing characteristic is peculiar to the wide area point-to-point networks. That is, the packets travel from one point to a sole destination. There is the absence of the *broadcast* capability where packets 'in flight' can be captured by all the nodes. Such broadcast networks are discussed in section 3.3. Other concerns are *flow control* and *congestion*. The network must not be flooded with packets to the extent that there is a severe degradation of system performance levels.

X.25

There are X.25 protocols for the operation of this layer between the DTE and DCE. It uses a virtual circuit system which involves explicit connection, data transfer and termination of connection phases.

Connection establishment begins when the DTE sends to its DCE a 'call request' packet addressed to the remote DTE. When the remote DCE receives this 'call request', it transmits an 'incoming call' packet to the DTE. The receiving DTE may either accept or reject the call (see Figure 3.12). Acceptance is indicated to the calling DTE by sending it a 'call accepted' packet, on receipt of which the virtual circuit is set up. Rejection or disconnection is indicated by transmitting a 'clear request' packet. Disconnection is complete when a 'clear confirmation' response is received from the node that was sent the 'clear request' (see Figure 3.13).

The information transfer uses a Go-Back-N ARQ protocol as discussed in section 3.2.2. The caller can specify the maximum packet length to be

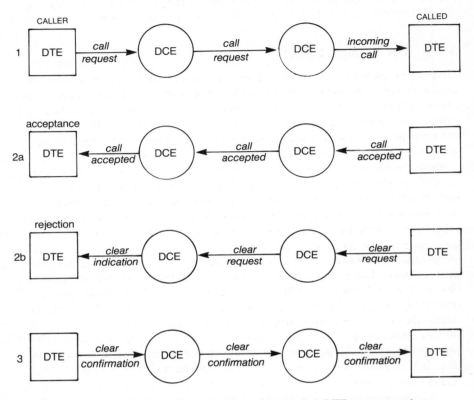

Fig. 3.12 X.25 connection establishment. The called DTE may accept or reject

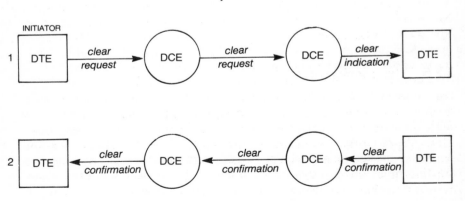

Fig. 3.13 X.25 disconnection protocol

used in the transmission. Possible maximum packet lengths allowed are 16, 32, 128, 256, 512 and 1024 bytes with 128 being the default.

3.2.4 The transport layer

This layer handles communication between individual processes at different hosts. A user operates within a process environment. Therefore, communication between users involves communication between processes. The transport layer is designed to support such interprocess communication. The protocols in this layer are therefore implemented only at hosts and not in the IMPs.

A network-wide addressing scheme which uniquely identifies not only all the processes offering some kind of service to the users of the network but also the valid user processes requesting any of those services is fundamental to this transport service. A mechanism employed in the mapping of service names to network addresses will be discussed in Chapter 5 under 'name servers'.

Before data transfer between processes begins, the sender process must request that a connection be established with the receiving process. On receipt by the sender of the 'connection accepted' indication from the receiving process, data transmission can commence. An explicit 'termination of connection' protocol ends the transmission.

The level of error checking and other controls will be determined by the type of service provided by the lower layers. If the network layer provides only a datagram service there will be a great deal more work at the transport layer in order to ensure the integrity of the messages received.

Many connections from one host to the same server process may be open at the same time. The receiving process may not be able to cope fast enough with all the incoming messages. In order to prevent the flooding of the receiver by fast incoming messages, buffering techniques and other flow control schemes must be employed.

3.2.5 The session layer

This need for processes to communicate, described in the previous section, must now be seen in the context of a task being divided into subtasks which may be mapped onto a number of different processes. Although more than one process may reside on one host, processes on remote hosts may be involved (see Figure 3.14). The session layer handles the interprocess communication between pairs of processes. This communication may involve only processes at the local host or it may be between a local host and remote host in which case the transport layer is needed.

When there is a long task to be performed, e.g. the transfer of a large file, it would be disastrous if a failure near the completion of the task

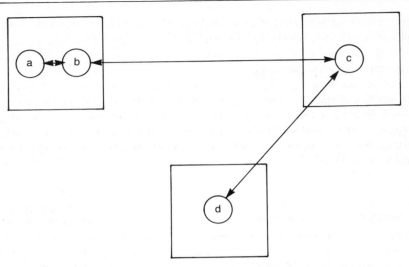

Fig. 3.14   A session involving 4 processes (a, b, c, d) at 3 hosts

necessitated a restart of the entire task. In order to avoid this, the session layer divides these tasks into subtasks and ensures that there is no repeat of completed subtasks. In doing this, there is an attempt to make failures below this layer transparent to higher layers.

3.2.6   The presentation layer

The major concerns at this layer are:

(a) to ensure that information remains semantically sound when trans-
    mitted to a remote host that uses different data storage forms (e.g.
    different character codes and word lengths);
(b) to permit terminals of varied types to use the network; and
(c) to provide an acceptable level of security and privacy to users of the
    network.

In short, the presentation layer handles the form in which data are presented to the network by the user, and delivered to the user by the network.

To achieve (a), there must be conversion, when necessary, of the data format used at a local host to the format used in the subnet for transmission through the net, followed by a conversion to the format used at the remote host before delivery.

Virtual terminal system
To achieve (b), we have to implement a *virtual terminal* system (see Figure 3.15). Think of the case where users will like to log onto an interactive

application that is located at a remote host. The designer of the interactive application has no knowledge of the kind of terminals that will be used. In fact, if the designer would like the facility to be widely used, he will have to accommodate a wide range of terminals.

The virtual terminal system involves the use of a data structure that represents a virtual terminal. A copy of this data structure will be located at the site that runs the interactive application and will be 'seen' by that program as the terminal. At each host, where there are terminals used as entry to the application, there will be a copy of the data structure for each terminal (see Figure 3.15).

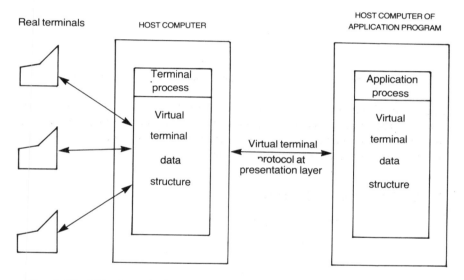

Fig. 3.15 Virtual terminal represented by data structure at the terminal end and at the application program end

At the application program end, there will be a process that manages that data structure and, similarly, the real terminal will have a terminal process managing its instance of the data structure. Communication between real terminals and the application program is via these processes which are implemented in the presentation layer of each host machine. A virtual terminal protocol specifies the interaction between the application process and the terminal process.

For example, the data structure should include a data item to accommodate different colors in the display. However, a terminal may have a monochrome monitor. The application program can update its virtual terminal with a certain choice of color. This is relayed to the terminal process which, in updating its data structure, may have to choose from reverse video and blinking. The terminal process will then modify the display of the real terminal based on its data structure.

Security and privacy

To achieve (c), the raw data are converted into some coded form before transmission through the net and this is followed by a decode operation at the destination host. The security of this system will depend on how difficult it is for an intruder to break the code. This is an area of serious concern because of the highly confidential nature of information that may be transmitted through the network.

Several cryptographic techniques have been employed but the *encryption* method, which involves the use of secret keys, seems most favorable. In this method the raw or *plaintext* is transformed by an algorithm which is driven by a *key* (a bit string usually known only by the sender and receiver). The output from this transformation, called the *ciphertext*, is transmitted and on arrival the recipient uses the key to *decrypt* the ciphertext back into plaintext.

Additional security can be introduced by having two keys for each communication. An encode or 'E' key can be used to convert the plaintext to ciphertext, and a separate key – the decode or 'D' key – can be used to convert the ciphertext back into plaintext. With such a system, a user can distribute his encode key to all from whom he expects coded information, and he keeps his decode key secret, thus ensuring that he is the only one who can understand the text. The encode key is called a public key hence such encryption systems are called *public key cryptographic systems*. For more details on *cryptography* see Tanenbaum (1981).

3.2.7   The application layer

This, the highest layer in the hierarchy, is the one with which the user interacts. To the user, the network provides several services. These services are designed to meet the users' application needs. These applications vary with users but some general common interests can be identified. Therefore, although there may not yet be any international standards available for this layer, there are certain applications which have been implemented on many networks.

Some of the popular applications are electronic mail, electronic funds transfers, file and job transfer systems, remote job entry, and public bulletin board and advertising systems.

Many of the applications can be categorized as distributed filing systems, distributed database systems and distributed computation systems. Working very closely with these application processes is the network or distributed operating system. Many of the issues involved in the design of these systems will be discussed later.

3.3 NETWORK TOPOLOGY

The *topology* of the network involves the location of IMPs, hosts and terminals and the existence of physical links between these devices. The performance levels achieved in the network are in some areas dependent on the network topology.

The effect on the network of a damaged line or a breakdown at some IMP or node is a major concern to the designer. There is also the question of cost and how best to minimize the cost without sacrificing too much on performance. Although some of the issues of topology may be the same for wide area and local area networks, there are sufficient differences to merit separate discussion.

3.3.1 Wide area networks

The aim in wide area networks is to provide services to users spread over a wide geographical area. There is little or no control over where the hosts or terminals will be located. The topological problem here is where to locate the IMPs (nodes) and lines so as to provide reliable service.

The extent of the demand for network services will differ with hosts. The volume of information traffic generated in the segments of the network will therefore vary with this demand. As a result of this varying demand, some hosts and terminals can be connected to *concentrators* rather than directly to the IMP. A concentrator accepts input from several lines and outputs information onto a single line, and in addition it can feed several lines off the input from that single line. Hence decisions must be made regarding not only the location of IMPs but also the location of concentrators and the choice of adequate channel capacity for the separate links.

The topology usually involves a hierarchical approach with a backbone system of IMPs and large capacity lines to which are connected clusters of concentrators serving the hosts or terminals (see Figure 3.16). One IMP can therefore serve a relatively large user population which will then be divided into smaller areas each served by a concentrator. However, where a host has a considerably higher demand for network services or enjoys some other special privilege that host can be linked directly to an IMP.

To provide an acceptable level of reliability, some redundancy must be built into the network, that is to say there must be multiple paths between nodes. Determining the level of redundancy can be aided by applying techniques from graph theory.

3.3.2 Local area networks

Local area networks occupy a limited physical range, usually an office building, manufacturing plant, university campus and similar single

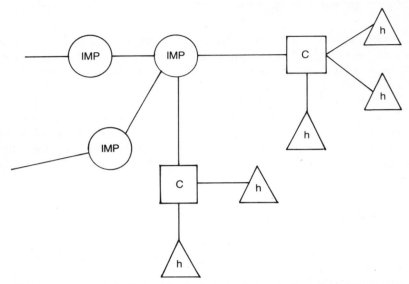

Fig. 3.16   A wide area network with hierarchical topology. Several hosts (h)
linked directly to a concentrator (C) and concentrators linked to an IMP

organizations. There is no communication subnet. The computing
elements (micro to mainframe computers, intelligent workstations, office
equipment) are connected directly to each other via the communication
link. These processing units are referred to as nodes or *stations*. The needs
of the various departments in the organization will determine the
location of these nodes. The decision on how to link them together follows
from this.

A few patterns have emerged offering different levels of performance
and reliability with the tradeoffs being simplicity and inexpensiveness.
However, it seems that, irrespective of the topology, an acceptable degree
of reliability can be achieved by upgrading the quality of the physical
medium and employing an efficient method for sharing the use of the
medium, i.e. the *access method*. A brief look at these patterns and the
access methods follows.

3.3.2.1   The bus

In the bus (see Figure 3.17a) a cable forms the backbone to which all the
stations are connected. Messages travel in both directions along the bus.
There are two major transmission techniques:

(a) *baseband* – digital signaling used with no modulation – in a broadcast environment, i.e. all the stations can hear the message transmitted; and

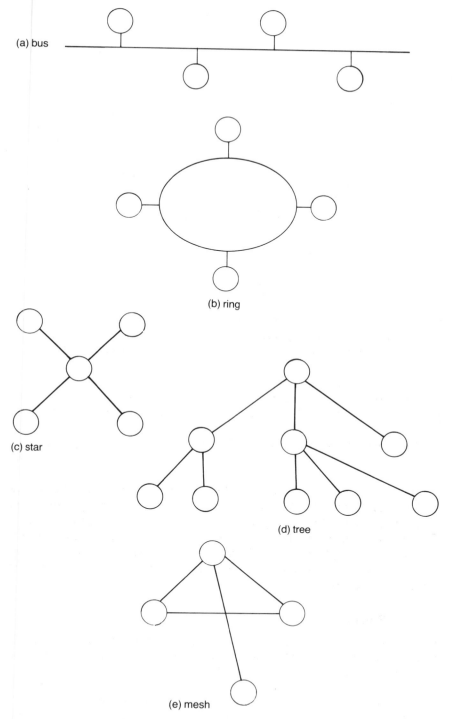

Fig. 3.17 Local area network topologies

(b) *broadband* in which there is modulation of the signal onto different frequency bands.

The baseband bus uses time division multiplexing to share the channel among the stations. This takes several different forms allowing different levels of performance. Some of these forms are *slotted ALOHA*, *carrier-sense multiple access* (CSMA), *carrier-sense multiple access with collision detection* (CSMA/CD) and *token access*.

Slotted ALOHA
In slotted ALOHA, time is divided into equal intervals called slots, one interval corresponding to the transmission time of a packet. Stations wishing to transmit must do so only at the beginning of a time slot. However, two stations can choose to transmit within the same time slot and therefore packets can collide. Stations wait for a positive acknowledgment from the destination station to determine that the packet has arrived. If no positive acknowledgment of receipt returns within a given time interval, the stations wait for some number of time slots and then retransmit.

Of course, collisions can occur again, but the number of collisions can be reduced if there is some statistical control over the transmission attempts. Slotted ALOHA is one of the access methods that are based on the pioneering work of the University of Hawaii's broadcast radio network, *ALOHA* (see Abramson, 1973). Another access method, *pure ALOHA*, allows the stations to transmit whenever they have packets to send. As the amount of traffic increases the number of collisions in pure ALOHA is, as expected, more than in slotted ALOHA. Hence the slotted technique is preferred.

CSMA
In CSMA, stations listen to the channel. If the channel is idle a station may transmit. Since other stations may transmit as long as they sense an idle channel, collisions can occur. If no positive acknowledgment is received within the time-out interval there will be further attempts to transmit.

If stations wishing to transmit find the channel busy, but continue listening to transmit as soon as the channel is idle, this is termed *1-persistent CSMA*, since stations transmit with a probability of 1 whenever they find that the channel is idle. There is also *p-persistent CSMA* where a station, on sensing that the channel is idle transmits with a probability p. A variation of this in which stations, having sensed a busy channel, do not continue to listen, but merely wait a random period of time then try again, is called *non-persistent CSMA*.

CSMA/CD
In CSMA/CD, the stations wishing to transmit do so after sensing that the channel is idle. However, they continue to listen to the channel in order to

detect a collision. If a collision occurs, transmission is stopped and will be attempted later. This access method was pioneered in the development of Ethernet, a popular local area network by the Xerox Corporation of the USA during the early 1970s (Metcalfe and Boggs, 1976). One advantage of this technique that should be immediately obvious is the reduction in the amount of bandwidth wasted due to collisions. Stations do not have to wait for a fixed interval of time before detecting a collision.

Token access
In token access, the use of the channel is dedicated to stations to transmit one packet. During that period only the station that has the privilege to transmit can do so. The *token* is a special packet that is passed from station to station. A station must wait until it receives the token before transmitting.

Broadband bus
In a broadband bus, FDM (see section 3.2.1) is used to share the channel bandwidth. Such LANs use a CATV broadband coaxial cable which permits multiple frequency channels multiplexed onto the single medium.

3.3.2.2 The ring
Messages travel in one direction around the ring (see Figure 3.17b). *Repeaters* are strategically positioned on the ring to propagate (repeat) the message, thus avoiding attenuation of the signal. Usually the station that sends a packet is responsible for removing it from the ring. The access methods include *empty slot*, *register insertion* and *token passing*.

Empty slot
In empty slot, a number of packets (possibly one) circulate around the ring. A station wishing to transmit must wait for an empty slot into which it places its packet of information. A popular local area ring network is the *Cambridge ring* (Needham, 1979; Wilkes and Needham, 1980) which was developed in the early 1970s at Cambridge University. It uses an empty slot access technique in which one fixed-size minipacket constantly circulates around the ring. The station that uses the slot must be the one to release it; this release must follow every single use even if that station has another packet to send. The empty slot becomes available to the next station on the ring and so on; hence, as long as a station has a packet to send, no other station can send two consecutive packets.

Register insertion
The register insertion technique usually involves the use of shift registers at the interface between each station and the ring. These registers can be switched in and out of circuit with the ring. One is used for output transmission and is switched into the ring, at an appropriate gap, when

there is a need to transmit. The other receives input from the ring. This input is either kept by the station if it is the right destination or is switched back into the ring.

Token passing

In token passing, a special bit sequence called a token circulates around the ring. This is the oldest and probably still the most popular ring network. Pioneering work in the token ring has been attributed to D.J. Farber and K.C. Larson (Tanenbaum, 1981). A station wishing to transmit must wait for the token. When it arrives, the token is seized by the station, the packet of information is placed onto the ring and the token is put back into circulation.

One important difference between the empty slot and token passing methods is that, in the latter case, if a neighboring station has information to send, it will see the token immediately following the packet of its upstream neighbor, seize the token and start transmitting its own packet. This removes the necessity of having to wait for a complete round trip as in the one empty slot technique. However, this wait time can be reduced in the empty slot system by having multiple empty slots.

3.3.2.3   The star

The star network (see Figure 3.17c) is the traditional approach used in connecting remote terminals to a central computer. This topology is therefore often preserved when upgrading the network. This upgrade may involve the connection of smaller processing stations to the much larger central operation. All access is directed through the central computer which makes the system very vulnerable to failures at the centre.

However, as a result of developments in the telephone industry, there now exists efficient, automatic digital switching exchanges which can work well as the hub in a star network. By using such a *PABX* (Private Automatic Branch Exchange) both telephone services and computer data transmission can be effectively handled by the same network.

3.3.2.4   The tree

A schematic of the tree network is shown in Figure 3.17d. However, the practical implementation of the tree as a LAN usually takes the form of several segments of a bus linked to a backbone bus (see Figure 3.18). The same access methods would apply as with the single bus. However, there are additional technical complexities introduced due to the use of cable connectors between the bus segments.

3.3.2.5   The mesh

The *mesh* topology (see Figure 3.17e) is not popular as a LAN system. This use of point-to-point links with sophisticated routing algorithms is a technique that can be employed in the communication subnet of wide area

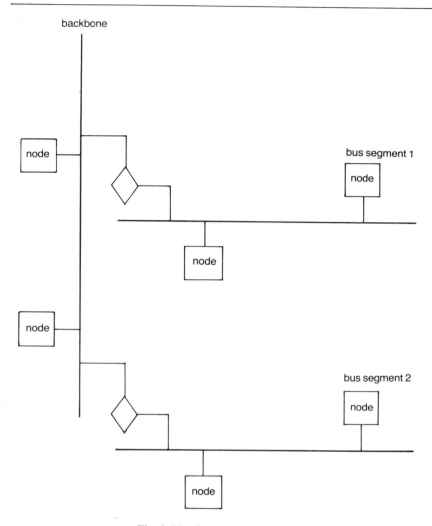

backbone

node

bus segment 1

node

node

node

bus segment 2

node

node

Fig. 3.18 A tree of bus segments

networks. The small geographical area covered by LANs usually lends itself to the implementation of simpler topologies such as the bus, ring and star.

3.4 NETWORK INTERCONNECTION

In order to extend even further the opportunities for information exchange, computer networks can be interconnected. To connect two networks, a computer is dedicated to the handling of the interface

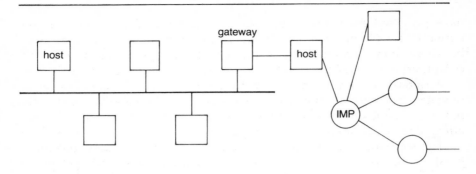

Fig. 3.19   A gateway connecting a LAN to a wide area network

between the two networks. This computer or communications processor is called a *gateway* (see Figure 3.19).

With the implementation of LANs becoming more common there will be increasing need to connect these to wide area networks. There are also reasons for connecting two long-haul networks. The protocols used on the two networks will, more often than not, be different. It is the function of the gateway to perform the protocol conversion. Packets addressed to the other network go to the gateway which converts them from the protocol of the sender's net to that of the receiver's. After the conversion, the packets will be relayed.

Since the gateway operates between the networks, the question of its ownership and maintenance must be resolved before implementation. One approach to this problem is the use of *half-gateways*. Instead of a single gateway, two half-gateways can be employed. Each of the two interconnected networks owns its half-gateway which is responsible for the conversion of information from its internal protocol to a standard internet protocol and *vice versa*.

It has been found that connecting two local networks each of the same topology is a useful strategy. In particular, ring LANs can be inter-connected to form a multiple ring and so provide efficient network service to a wider range of users. Each component ring is usually called a *petal*. In such a system, access from one petal to the other is via a dedicated processor called a *bridge*. One advantage of this system is that some network failures can be isolated to the petal in which they occur rather than putting the whole network out of operation.

3.5   SUMMARY

Computer networks have materialized because of the technological strides made in communications. The developments made in microelectronics have provided even further opportunities for linking computers in a network. Telephone communications, although mainly analog, form the backbone of many computer networks. The digital signals transmitted by computers are modulated in order to be carried by the analog channels.

An alternative approach is to map the digital values onto distinct levels of voltage and current, thus removing the need to modulate. This method has been adopted widely in LAN technology and has proven sufficiently efficient to be considered as a technique for transmitting voice signals.

Transmission media used in computer communications include twisted pair, coaxial cable, optical fibers, radio frequencies and satellites. Several methods, categorized as time division multiplexing and frequency division multiplexing, have been employed to share the communications channel. Furthermore, there is the choice of circuit switching and packet switching techniques.

The ISO has proposed a seven-layer model for the design of computer networks. The proposal addresses issues from the physical media to the user applications environment. The aim is to achieve a common standard in network design which would facilitate extension and interconnection.

Issues regarding performance, reliability, simplicity and cost arise when choosing the network topology. Some simple patterns have emerged in LAN design. Those that are in common use are the bus, ring and star networks. The use of a hierarchical structure seems popular among the wide area networks. Networks of different architectures can be linked by using a dedicated communications processor called a gateway; while a bridge is used to link LANs that are of the same topology.

3.6 QUESTIONS

3.1 How does information transmitted by a computer differ from that of vocal communication?

3.2 Explain the difference between the baud rate of a channel and the number of bits per second transmitted by that channel.

3.3 Calculate the channel capacity of a channel which has a bandwidth of 10 kHz and a dB value of 30.

3.4 Why is Nyquist's theorem not a sufficient indicator of channel capacity?

3.5 What is modulation? Describe three modulation techniques.

3.6 Compare and contrast the following transmission media:

(a) twisted pair and coaxial cable,
(b) coaxial cable and optical fibers,
(c) terrestrial links and satellite.

3.7 Name the seven layers in the ISO Reference model. Give a rationale for a layered approach to network architecture.

3.8 What role does CCITT play in the specification of standards for computer communications?

3.9 Briefly indicate the major issues at each of the layers of the reference model for OSI.

3.10 Distinguish between time division multiplexing and frequency division multiplexing. Suggest any advantages that you think one technique has over the other.

3.11 Why is the packet switching technique more suitable than circuit switching for computer communications?

3.12 Describe a flow control system that is implementable at the data link layer.

3.13 Distinguish between the virtual call and the datagram service at the network layer. Indicate any advantages that each enjoys over the other.

3.14 What differences are there between a wide area network and a local area network?

3.15 What channel access methods have been used on a local area bus network?

3.16 What channel access methods have been used on a local area ring network?

3.17 How would a token access bus differ from a token passing ring network?

3.18 Imagine that you had to choose a LAN for your office building. What factors would you take into consideration in making your choice?

3.19 If the bit rate on a ring is 10 Mbps and the signal propagation speed of the channel is 200 m/microsec. How long should the ring be in order to hold an entire 8-bit token?

3.20 Indicate the steps that you would take to design

  (i) a bridge, and

  (ii) a gateway, to connect two networks.

3.7 REFERENCES

1 Abramson, N., 1973. 'The ALOHA system', In *Computer-Communication Networks*, eds N. Abramson & F. Kuo, Englewood Cliffs: Prentice Hall.
2 Cole, R., 1981. *Computer Communications*, London: Macmillan Press.
3 Davies, D.W. and Barber, D.L.A., 1973. *Communication Networks for Computers*. London: John Wiley & Sons.
4 Davies, D.W. et al, 1979. *Computer Networks and their Protocols*. Chichester: John Wiley & Sons.
5 Digital, 1985. *Networks and Communications Buyer's Guide*, October to December Edition, Digital Equipment Corporation.
6 Gee, K.C.E., 1983. *Introduction to Local Area Computer Networks*. London: Macmillan Press.
7 Metcalfe, R.M. and Boggs, D.R., 1976. 'Ethernet: Distributed Packet Switching

for local computer networks', Communications of the A.C.M., **19**, 7, Jul., 395–404.

8 Needham, R.M., 1979. System aspects of the Cambridge Ring, Proceedings of the Seventh Symposium on Operating System Principles, ACM, 82–85: Pacific Grove, California.

9 Tanenbaum, A.S., 1981. *Computer Networks*, Englewood Cliffs: Prentice Hall.

10 U.K. Post Office, 1975. *Handbook of Data Communications*, NCC Publications.

11 Wilkes, M.V. and Needham, R.M., 1980. 'The Cambridge Model Distributed System', *ACM SIGOPS, Operating Systems Review*, **14**, 1, 21–29.

CHAPTER FOUR

OPERATING SYSTEMS FOR DISTRIBUTED AND PARALLEL COMPUTING

The *operating system* manages the computer resources with the objective of trying to meet, in as satisfactory a manner as possible, the requirements of users of the system. The resources that are managed by the operating system include not only the bare hardware components but certain software elements as well. The hardware resources usually fall into the following categories: central processing units, input/output processing units, primary and secondary storage units, and peripheral input/output devices. Common software entities managed by the system are processes and files. User requirements can range from playing games on a personal microcomputer to solving large-scale scientific problems on super-computers.

We saw in Chapter 2 that many supercomputers are being built to allow parallelism in program execution. However, without a suitable operating system, optimum use cannot be made of the many processors and other hardware resources that these systems possess. The parallel strands in the user jobs have to be identified. The allocation of processors and other resources follows from this. In addition, there has to be an effective mechanism for synchronizing the activity among the parallel strands. Indeed, the operating system will have a considerable effect on the level of performance of the parallel computer system.

In the computer network environment, there is the additional resource of the network itself. In Chapter 3 we saw how a layered architecture can be used for network design. Each host in the network will have its own implementation of the protocols at each layer. One can therefore view these protocol handlers as additions to the operating system at each host computer.

One of the aims of the network design is to offer services, to as many users as possible, irrespective of where they are located. Therefore, not only is there the task of handling local user requirements, but there is also the responsibility to serve the needs of remote users. The system must be able to identify and locate the different services offered on the network. Access to these services will have to be controlled to prevent unauthorized access to selective services, hence some user validation mechanism must be employed. There must also be some facility for charging users for the services received from the network. These are only some of the issues which the operating system designer must address.

Since networks link computers which may be from different manufacturers, it follows that each host may have a different operating system. These operating systems will manage the local resources without any knowledge of the network. It is therefore necessary either to add to each local operating system a process which will act as the interface with the network, or to replace the separate heterogeneous operating systems by one homogeneous system.

That process which acts as the interface between the host and the net in the heterogeneous environment is called the *agent process*. The collection of agent processes is called a *network operating system*. The homogeneous network-wide operating system is called a *distributed operating system*. These two approaches present different design and implementation problems, aspects of which we will discuss in the next two sections. Following this, we will look briefly at the parallel computer system.

4.1 NETWORK OPERATING SYSTEMS

The use of heterogeneous hardware systems in computer networks is in many cases a positive feature. Indeed, in long-haul networks it is difficult to conceive of popular use if different computers could not hook onto the network. There is, therefore, the inevitable presence of different operating systems. The design of a network operating system to permit the running at hosts of their local operating systems is an understandable approach. This design must provide a *command language* to accommodate user requests for network service, and the *agent process* to accept these network commands and pass them along to the appropriate network sites.

4.1.1 Command language

Users communicate with the operating system by issuing commands, e.g. 'run job'. These commands, which are elements of the command language, are intercepted by the *command interpreter/processor* which usually occupies the highest layer of the operating system hierarchy (see Figure 4.1). In some cases, the command processor is implemented as a user process and not part of the operating system. These commands may be explicit ones which are separate from the program language code, or they may be implicit entries in the program language code which are implemented as system calls.

In order to provide network services to the user, a set of commands must be furnished to allow access to these services. If the network provides a file transfer facility, for example, there will be some command to allow the use of this facility. The command must be distinguishable from the commands used by the local operating system.

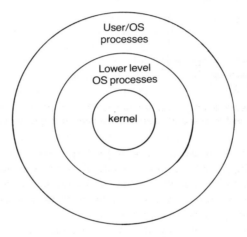

Fig. 4.1   An operating system hierarchy

However, the system may be designed to hide the differences in the commands from the user. In the case where a service can be provided locally as well as by a remote site, the same command name may be used. Using the same example as above, a transfer file operation from one site to another can be viewed as a special case of a copy file command. Hence one command name, e.g. 'copy', can be used for both the completely local copy operation and the one which involves a remote site. The argument list will determine the sites involved. The specification of the arguments will involve decisions on how many, what names and what format must be used. The level of *transparency* is again a matter of concern, i.e. what is the extent of the users' awareness of the network?

Assume that the command, 'copy fromfile, tofile', means that the system determines the location of the file, 'fromfile', then copies it to a file called 'tofile' at the local host. The responsibility for finding the name and the address of the host at which 'fromfile' resides is that of the system. This

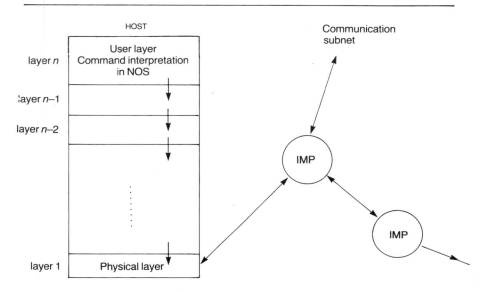

Fig. 4.2 The network operating system (NOS) interprets commands then sends them onto the net via the lower layer protocols

would involve the keeping of sufficiently large databases to supply the necessary mapping from local to global file naming. On the other hand, a command form may be used which requires knowledge by the user of the location of 'fromfile', in which case the user supplies the pathname for the file, e.g. 'host/user/project/filename'.

Commands to the network may also be embedded within the user program for execution at run time. A user process may be allowed, at run time, to create other processes (child processes) that are to be run on remote hosts in a distributed computing environment. For example, the command

fork (host/user/filename, host)

may require that the load image of a process be obtained from the named file, and created and run at the host given in the second parameter.

The responsibility of the network operating system is to trap such network commands, interpret them and then pass them on to the lower layers of the network protocol (see Figure 4.2).

4.1.2 The agent process

In a network with heterogeneous operating systems, each host will be allowed entry to the network services by an agent process. Commands will be filtered out of the set of user commands – local and remote – and directed to the agent process (see Figure 4.3).

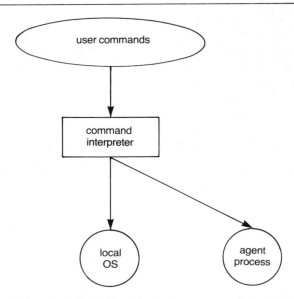

Fig. 4.3 Commands are filtered to agent process or local OS

In order to understand the function of the agent process, consider the commands in terms of the three parameters: *user*, *remote host* and *task*. The agent must maintain databases showing the relations between these parameters. For each valid user, there must be an indication of the hosts to which access is allowed, the log-on information, the nature of tasks permitted, accounting information and such like (see Figure 4.4).

One major category of network tasks at the operating system level is *file management*. The network should give users the facility to access files, subject to proper authorization, at remote hosts. The accessing of files can be done in a location transparent manner or the users may be fully aware of the location of the files being accessed.

Where the user is in full control, then the agent process may be supplied with a complete textual pathname of the file. In this case, the agent needs only to perform the mapping from the textual host name to host address, while the remote operating system will complete the mapping from the other textual parameters – user, project, filename.

Where some degree of location transparency is supported, the agent will have to maintain a directory system of its own. There may be a fixed set of files that are available, via the agent, for the users of the network. This set may consist of common utility procedures, viz numerical algorithms, sort routines, etc. The users need not know where they are stored. The user merely names the file with a single textual parameter, e.g. 'run eigenvalue(datafile)', and the agent finds 'eigenvalue'.

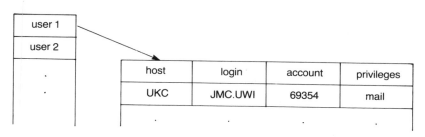

Fig. 4.4 Database for log in to remote host

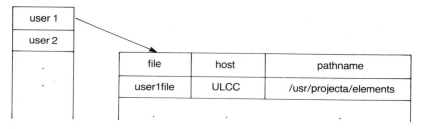

Fig. 4.5 Database relating users to their remote files

On the other hand, there may be the facility for managing all the files – user and system – in the network in this location-transparent manner. Here we are thinking in terms of the features provided by some file server systems. These will be discussed in Chapter 5.

However, the agent may support an environment where, for each interested user, a directory entry is made for all the remote files that that user requires access to (Tanenbaum, 1981). The agent process may be designed to hide file naming and other local conventions from the remote user. To achieve this, the agent process may provide its own file name to which the users refer. This virtual file name is then mapped onto the actual host and file name. This mapping is made possible by maintaining a file database with the relevant entries (see Figure 4.5).

When implementing the agent, one has to determine:

(a) the mechanism for interaction with the local operating system; and
(b) the location of the agent relative to the host's operating system.

Interaction with the local operating system
Traditional operating system architecture includes a number of processes running on top of a *kernel*. The kernel is responsible for process scheduling, context switching, interaction with I/O devices and other lower level functions. System calls are usually the vehicle used by the processes in interacting with the kernel. The system call is one instance of

the common procedure call mechanism (see section 4.2.2). Where the local operating system uses this method, *procedure calls* will be the means of interaction with the agent. Therefore, in order to communicate with the agent, a call is issued which causes entry to the agent procedure. On completion of the agent procedure, there is an exit to the caller.

Another communication technique is *message passing*. In fact, this is the way in which communication across a network is accomplished. The agent sends messages to and receives messages from remote hosts. If the local operating system uses message passing then it follows that the communication interface between the local host and agent will be somewhat compatible with that between the agent and the network.

Both of these techniques will be examined in greater detail in section 4.2.2. It is sufficient to say here that it is felt that the interface with the local operating system can be established with relatively less difficulty if that local system embodies a message passing inter-process communication scheme.

The siting of the agent process
There still remains the question of where to locate the agent relative to the local operating system. Three alternative approaches have been suggested (Collinson, 1984). These are:

(a) the agent may be implemented as a user process at the host;
(b) it may be implemented as part of the kernel of the local operating system; or
(c) it may be placed in a separate machine.

Figure 4.6 shows the agent as a user process. Notice that all communication between other user processes and the agent must go via the kernel. This means that, for example, when a user process sends a message onto the network it passes across the user/kernel boundary three times − first there is the system call (or send message) from user to agent, secondly there is the relaying of the message to the agent, and thirdly there is the transfer from the agent to the lower layers of the network protocol which reside in the kernel. This could slow down the response to the users of the network. This situation could be made worse if the agent, being a user process, can be swapped out of primary storage. However, this technique is advantageous in that it does not increase the kernel size significantly.

Figure 4.7 shows the agent implemented as part of the kernel. This arrangement avoids some of the traffic generated in technique (a). However the size of the kernel is significantly increased. This may not be tolerable on small host machines.

The agent may reside at a separate machine (see Figure 4.8). In this case, the agent processor may contain a collection of modules each of which interfaces with an operating system from a particular host. With

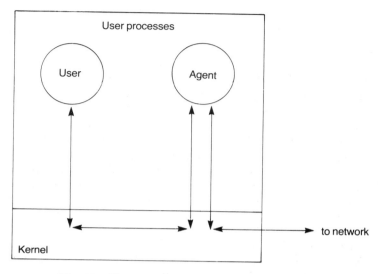

Fig. 4.6 The agent as a user process

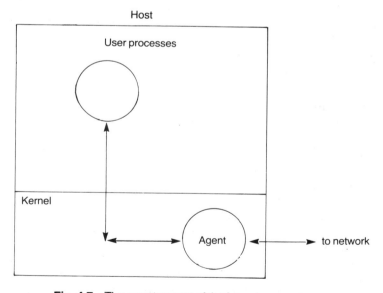

Fig. 4.7 The agent as part of the kernel

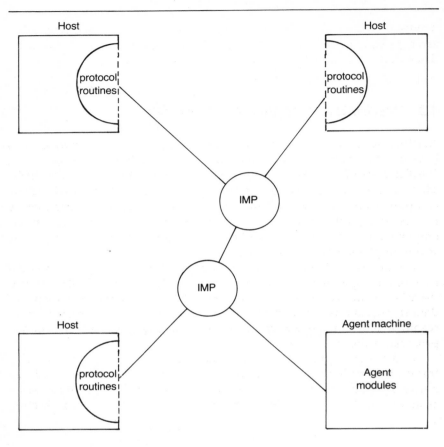

Fig. 4.8   The agent at a separate machine

this arrangement all network accesses from these hosts will be via the agent machine. It will still be necessary to have lower layer network protocol routines at the individual hosts to:

(a) send the uninterpreted commands to the agent machine; and
(b) receive messages from the agent.

However, the network service will be vulnerable to failures at the agent machine. The storage of all the relevant data and control information at this single machine simplifies the implementation and management. On the other hand, the range of services provided by the agent may be restricted. In fact, this type of arrangement may be feasible only if some limited network service such as file storage and retrieval is provided by the agent. If that is the case then we can have other agents being implemented at other machines to provide other services. Since each of these agents needs software routines to run on its behalf at the user machines, this arrangement can be classified as a client-server system which will be discussed in Chapter 5.

4.2 DISTRIBUTED OPERATING SYSTEMS

Another approach to the design of operating systems for networks is to have one operating system for the whole network. This operating system is called a *distributed operating system* (Tanenbaum and Van Renesse, 1985). This method is used, so far, mainly in local area networks where the computers are usually from the same manufacturer and consequently possess compatible hardware features. Although this approach can be employed in wide area networks, the diversity of machines presents severe implementation difficulties.

The key objective in the design of a distributed operating system is network transparency, i.e. the user of the network operates at all times as if there is only one computer – the local host. The operating system manages data storage and retrieval, data and program migration, load distribution, resource allocation, etc. without the user being aware of all the separate processing sites involved.

Two design approaches have been identified. One approach is to take a traditional, multiprogramming, uniprocessor operating system and add network capabilities to it. The other approach is to design a new operating system from scratch. Examples of both approaches are given in section 4.2.4.

4.2.1 Some problems

In addition to the fundamental problems of concurrent operation and synchronous and asynchronous processing, there are the particular problems of a network environment. The following four points are of major concern:

(a) that the integrity of data transferred and stored should be preserved;
(b) that fail-soft operation in the face of possible crashes at remote processing sites should be ensured;
(c) the provision of a high level of security against unwanted intrusions; and
(d) that an overall level of performance (response times, resource availability, etc.) that is acceptable to the users should be offered.

Integrity
The error handling mechanisms in the lowest layers of the network architecture and the reliable service provided by the physical

communications network can go a long way towards ensuring the correctness of the information transmitted. The use of compatible machinery in the network provides an environment where the data representations used across the network are the same, thus removing the need to perform data conversions. However, additional communication protocols might be necessary in order to ensure that commands sent across the network are effectively handled. There must be some certainty that a data area at a remote site is appropriately updated when such a request is made. The usual strategy here is never to assume anything, always seek a response or an acknowledgment.

Fail-soft operation

For *fail-soft operation* we need to incorporate some recovery features into the software. A systematic use of back-up and logging mechanisms must be adopted. There is the possibility that some failure can occur in the midst of updating a data area, such as a *file map*. The operating system should include measures to effect speedy recovery.

Privacy and security

The network allows a number of facilities to be shared among a large user public. Among these facilities will be resources which should only be accessed by users who belong to some privileged class. These privileged users must be able to feel that the resources which they own are held reasonably securely against loss and intrusion.

Performance

Performance levels are affected, not only by the hardware, but also by the software environment. The way in which information is stored affects retrieval times. The choice of mapping algorithms to convert textual names into absolute addresses is of great importance. The distribution of system control data areas like directories must also be given serious consideration. A poor choice of primary and secondary storage organization methods can result in considerably lowered performance levels.

Many of the pertinent communication issues have been introduced in Chapter 3. The areas which can fall under file management, and information storage and retrieval will be amplified in Chapters 5 and 6.

Two of the major distinguishing features in the design of distributed operating systems are:

(a) the way in which processes communicate with each other; and
(b) the control of access to shared resources.

We will now look at these features.

4.2.2 Interprocess communication

The interprocess communication system can be modeled along one of two basic forms. First there is the *procedure call* mechanism, and secondly there is the *message passing* scheme (Ball et al, 1979; Donnelley, 1980).

Procedure call

In *procedure call*, the calling process issues a call instruction naming the called process. Arguments are passed by value or reference to the called process. If both the caller and the called are running in user mode on the same machine, they could be procedures linked together in the same object module. Therefore, the call would involve a jump in execution from one procedure to the other, followed some time after by a return, without the need to enter the kernel of the operating system.

On the other hand, the call may require entry to the kernel, e.g., the called process may be an I/O handler which needs explicit operating system control. The call instruction is, in this case, a system call which causes the entry to the operating system kernel. The kernel transfers the arguments to the address space of the called process. The caller is forced to wait until the called process executes and then replies via the kernel to the calling process.

Remote procedure call

If the called process resides at a remote site, the arguments must be packaged as a message and transmitted through the network to the destination host, where it is executed as a procedure call, while the caller waits. On completion, the response is relayed back to the caller. This scheme is referred to as a *remote procedure call* (RPC) system.

Birrell and Nelson (1984) have indicated that the RPC mechanism has a number of attractive properties. They claim that it is based on a well-known technique that is relatively clean and simple; therefore, with RPC, it should be easier to support reliable distributed computation systems. The simplicity should generate an efficiency in design which would provide rapid exchange of information.

Five modules interact in the implementation of an RPC system. They are the user, the user-stub, the RPC communications package, the server-stub, and the server (see Figure 4.9). The RPC communications package is known as RPCRuntime.

The user-stub is invoked when the user makes a remote call. This resembles a normal local call. The user-stub assembles one or more packets which will include the target procedure and arguments, and then requests the local instance of RPCRuntime to transmit to the called machine. The remote RPCRuntime receives the packets and passes them to the server-stub. The server-stub unpacks and procedure calls the server. During this time, the user who issued the call waits. When the server has finished, the results are relayed via the same path. These five separate program modules allow independent development of these cooperating parts of the RPC system.

The RPC facility discussed by Birrell and Nelson allows users to access servers located anywhere in a large internet of more than a hundred Ethernets. Hence an efficient strategy for naming and locating servers must be employed. A distributed database system (see Chapter 6) is used to record these names and addresses. The RPCRuntime can access the database for the network address of some named service. A service has a two-parameter name. One parameter for type. e.g. file access, and a second parameter for a particular instance of that type. This allows individual user needs to be met within some category of service.

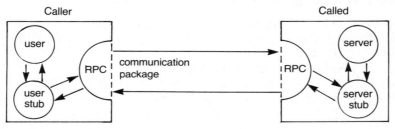

Fig. 4.9 A remote procedure call system with five modules. Adapted from Birrell, A.D. and Nelson, R.J., 1984, 'Implementing Remote Procedure Calls', *ACM Trans. Comput. Syst.*, **2**, 1(Feb), Copyright 1984, Association for Computing Machinery, Inc.

Message passing

In a *message passing* scheme, all communication is handled as message blocks which the kernel undertakes to transfer from a sender process to a receiver process. The kernel may store the message in intermediary buffers before delivering it to the receiver process. The sender process issues a 'send message' command in which it identifies the receiver and the message. The receiver usually must issue an explicit 'receive message' command in which it identifies a sender and names a data area in its address space for the deposit of the message.

The issuing of a 'send message' command is not a guarantee of receipt unless there is a specific protocol that provides this guarantee. Issuing of a 'receive message' command may not mean that a message has been sent. Whether the sender waits on the complete handling of the communication can be determined by the nature of the particular task and not upon the fact that a message passing instruction was issued. No blocking increases the parallelism in execution, but it also increases the programmers' responsibility to ensure correctness. Therefore, some blocking on the sender and receiver processes may be included in the message passing protocol. Message passing lends itself to easy extension to working in a distributed environment.

In Chapter 7, we will look at many parallel language projects which have as one of their objectives an improved environment for interprocess communication in distributed and parallel computing.

4.2.3 Resource sharing

Sharing is one of the main objectives for building a computer network. However, this sharing of resources is not a new issue. This has been an area of concern since the early days of multiprogramming operating system design. Hence there are many techniques that have been tried and, in some cases, proven in the development and production environments. Some of the problems are:

(a) how to deal with the contention for shared resources;
(b) how to synchronize activity to ensure that shared data areas are always left in a consistent state;
(c) how to schedule and allocate the resources;
(d) what the type and extent of access to a particular resource will be;
(e) how to authenticate the requesting user; and
(f) what is to be done when a resource becomes unavailable.

Contention and synchronization problems are handled by some locking mechanism which shuts out the use of the resource to all but a single user (or group of users). It is a rather common and effective tool used in the centralized environment. The communication scheme can also provide synchronization (see Chapter 7). In the distributed environment, complications are introduced since a user may require a collection of resources each of which is stored separately with distributed control, e.g. a distributed database (see Chapter 6).

In considering scheduling and allocation, we can distinguish between two cases:

(a) the resource belongs to a pool of identical resources; or
(b) there is only one instance of the resource.

In the case where the resource is one of a pool, state information can be held centrally on the members of the pool. Any available member can be allocated to a requesting user based on a first come, first served discipline or a priority scheme that involves some characteristic of the user. The objectives will determine the scheme, and it is sometimes necessary to strike a comfortable balance between conflicting objectives. For example, minimizing the communication cost can be at odds with increasing the parallelism in execution.

In order to minimize communication cost, it will be necessary always to try to allocate local resources or those nearest to the requesting site. On the other hand, an increase in parallelism may only be possible by increasing the level of distribution.

These concerns may be adequate for a hardware pool such as a pool of processors, but if the resource belongs to a software pool, e.g. several copies of a file, replicated system tables, or a distributed database, particular attention has to be paid to the preservation of the overall consistency of the stored information.

The resource may be a single object, e.g. a single-copy file, or a special purpose processor. Concurrent multiuser operation can be scheduled for the processor. Multiple readers can be permitted to the file, but a writer should be allowed exclusive access. If the file can be divided into several parts (pages) and concurrent access permitted to these distinct parts, then scheduling and allocation become more complex (see section 5.1).

Before a resource can be allocated to a user, that user should be required to demonstrate to the system that he/she possesses some right of access. Such an authentication scheme usually involves user ID and password with stored access control lists or matrices. The user provides a textual data item (a name) and the system compares it against some stored list of valid users for the particular resource. Privileges can be withdrawn by deleting one's 'name' from the list. Of course, an intruder need only present a valid 'name' and access is granted.

When a resource becomes unavailable, the user can be switched to an alternative, if one exists. If there is no alternative, then services must be curtailed until the restoration of the facility. Switching to alternative resources can introduce complications. This matter is discussed under 'partition failures' in section 6.5.

An approach to operating system design that provides, among other things, an elegant strategy for resource sharing is the *object model*. In the object model the resources of the system are abstracted as *objects*. Access to an object is restricted to those users who possess a *capability* for that object, e.g. a user cannot read a file unless that user possesses the capability for such action.

The capability is a unique name or pointer generated and protected by the system. The capability is allocated to the user to be used in accessing the object. Associated with each capability are the access rights given to the user of that capability. Several capabilities can exist for one object, thus permitting different privileges to users. All operations on capabilities are protected, so as to prevent unauthorized access to objects. Some notable object-oriented operating system projects are HYDRA (Wulf et al, 1974), CAP (Wilkes and Needham, 1979) and STAROS (Jones et al, 1979).

4.2.4 Example systems

In this section we will look at some distributed operating systems in order to appreciate the techniques used in facing some of the issues that have been highlighted. We will look first at two distributed kernels, then two distributed systems with more than kernel facilities, and finally two projects that are related to UNIX.

Accent

Carnegie–Mellon's Accent (Rashid and Robertson, 1981) is a message-passing kernel built to support a distributed computing environment. It allows flexible and transparent access to resources in the network. It is claimed to be a 'communication oriented' operating system, since its basic organizing principle is the abstraction of communication between processes.

Each host machine has an operating system kernel upon which sits a collection of processes (see Figure 4.10). The kernel handles, among other things, process management and interprocess communication (IPC). This IPC facility affords communication among processes within a local host and, via processes called 'network servers', communication with processes at remote hosts in the network.

Accent uses the concept of a *port* for the transport of messages. Access to services and facilities provided by a process is through a port. Messages may be sent to and received from these ports which are controlled by the kernel (see Figure 4.11). A queue of messages can be formed at a port and each message will be handled or removed in turn. Sender processes are not automatically blocked on sending a message, and the receipt of messages is basically asynchronous.

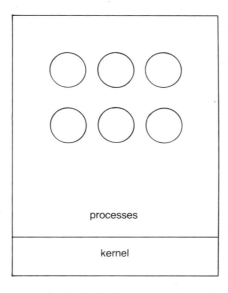

processes

kernel

Fig. 4.10 Process model of a distributed operating system at host

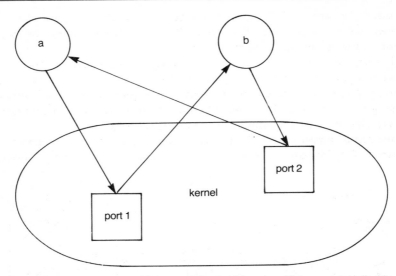

Fig. 4.11   Processes *a* and *b* communicate via ports which are controlled by
the OS kernel

The server process must, therefore, first create a port through which the user processes can gain access to the service it provides. This port creation is achieved through an 'AllocatePort' system call which, in effect, gives a local port name to that port and ownership of that port to the creator process. Before another process can remove a message from that port, it must be granted 'receive access' to it. This receive access cannot be shared, but it can be passed to another process through a message.

The initial owner of the port has receive access to it. Ownership can be passed to (but not shared with) another process. A port can be destroyed by a process only if that process is the owner of the port and also possesses receive access to it. This destruction is achieved by issuing a 'DeallocatePort' system call. If a process with only ownership of, or only receive access to, the port issues this system call, the port is not destroyed. That process's right (ownership or receive access) is given to the process that possesses the other right, and so both ownership and receive access now belong to the other process.

On the creation of a process, it is allowed access to two ports for message passing to and from the kernel. One of these ports is called the 'kernel port' to which the created process has send rights, and the kernel has receive rights. Therefore the process can send messages to the kernel through this port. The other port is called the 'data port' to which the process has receive access and the kernel has send rights, hence the kernel can send messages to the process through this port.

The parent of a process can ask that its access rights to ports be given to the child process. Access rights to the 'kernel' and 'data' ports of the child process can also be given to the parent. In this way parent-child communication is supported by the same basic port mechanism.

Emergency messages are used to communicate errors and other matters which require immediate action. These messages have high priority and are therefore allowed to jump the queue at a port. One of the messages conveyed in this way is the notification of the destruction of a port to all processes that still have access to that port.

Communication across the network involves the 'network server' (see Figure 4.12). Messages destined for a remote host are sent to the port

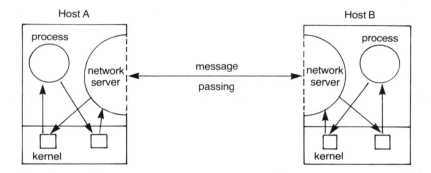

Fig. 4.12 Messages to a remote host are sent to the port owned by the network server. The network server sends messages to the port of the receiving process. Adapted from Rashid, R.F. and Robertson, G.G., 1981. 'Accent: A communication oriented network operating system kernel', *Proceedings of the eighth ACM Symposium on Operating Systems Principles, SIGOPS OSR*, **15**, 5, 64–75, Copyright 1981, Association for Computing Machinery, Inc.

which belongs to the local 'network server'. This 'network server' sends the message to the 'network server' at the remote host. The remote 'network server' has the responsibility of sending the message to the port of the receiving process.

The V kernel
The V kernel is a distributed operating system project undertaken at Stanford University (Cheriton, 1984; Tanenbaum and Van Renesse, 1985). The V system consists of a collection of workstations at each of which resides an identical copy of the V kernel.

The kernel is designed to support a client-server network model (see Chapter 5). It contains an interprocess communication handler, a kernel server for memory management and other basic services, and a device server which provides uniform access to I/O devices.

Each processor functions either as a server or a user workstation. Therefore there is no dynamic allocation of processors. The kernel on each processor manages its local processes which run concurrently and can, via the interprocess communication handler, send and receive messages across the network.

Each process has a unique 32-bit pid which is the address used in communication. A server can have a symbolic name which is registered with its kernel and can subsequently be used by requesting clients. When a client uses such a name, the client's kernel must broadcast this name to all the other kernels in order to locate the server. The (server-name, pid) pair is then put in a cache for future references.

In order to access a server, a client issues a 'SEND (message, pid)' and then blocks until it receives a reply from the server. Servers use 'RECEIVE' which provide a message buffer to accommodate the incoming message; and 'REPLY' which overwrites the message of the sender client.

One of the servers implemented to run on top of the V kernel is a central file server. It is viewed as just an ordinary user program. Most of the workstations do not have a disk, therefore this file server handles all the usual file system functions. It uses a hierarchical file system with each file having a UNIX-like file descriptor. A file is an object with a unique object identifier upon which can be mapped a symbolic name. Symbolic names exist in some 'context' which is similar to the concept of being in a directory. Given the 'context' and the symbolic name, the object identifier can be obtained.

Amoeba

Amoeba is another distributed operating system which embodies message passing and ports (Tanenbaum and Mullender, 1981; Tanenbaum and Van Renesse, 1985). The facilities or resources in the network – hardware and software – are classified as 'services' and each service is managed by one or more server processes. Services can be public such as disk service, file service, database service, etc. Such services are considered to be long-lived in that they are operable for most if not all of the time. There are also short-lived private services which are created to meet specific program needs.

A service is accessed through one or more ports. To receive service a message must be sent to one of the ports of the server process. Knowledge of the port number gives a process send access to that port. A process can accept messages from (i.e. listen to) all the ports that it owns.

The creation of processes is handled by a 'process server', which can be implemented as a user process or it can reside in the kernel. In Amoeba, the kernel contains the physical, data link and monitor layers. The physical and data link layers (see Chapter 3) are not part of the Amoeba design. The 'monitor layer' is the name Amoeba uses to refer to the software that handles port addressing and low-level process management.

Above the monitor layer is a transport layer (see Figure 4.13) which issues commands to the monitor layer to send messages to named ports. The monitor layer maps the ports onto machine addresses, packets the messages and sends it onto the network using a datagram service. The monitor is also responsible for the initiation and migration of processes.

The transport layer supports a transaction-oriented communication style, i.e each request to a server must be self contained. Basic transport primitives for users are 'send a request', 'receive a reply'. For servers there are 'accept a request', and 'send a reply'. The user/client blocks after sending until the server returns a reply.

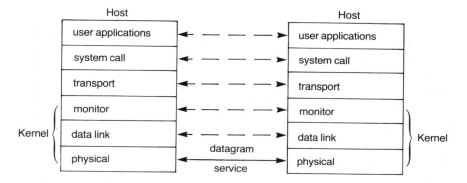

Fig. 4.13 The Amoeba layered architecture. Adapted from Tanenbaum, A.S. and Mullender, S., 1981, 'An overview of the Amoeba Distributed Operating System', *ACM SIGOPS OSR*, **15**, 3(July), 51–64, Copyright 1981, Association for Computing Machinery, Inc.

The system call layer is the interface between user programs and the operating system. Users have a number of routines which they can call to get system service, e.g. open file, read file, write file, etc. The highest layer is the user layer where user programs run.

A 'process server' creates a process in response to a 'create process' message which it receives on its port. The create process message is a process descriptor sent by the parent process for a child process. The process descriptor includes ports inherited from the parent, the CPU type and option required in order to facilitate allocation within the distributed system, the port from which to fetch the binary image of the process, and other relevant details. This process descriptor can be sent to the monitor on any machine willing and able to run the process.

Ports are manipulated directly by the user processes. The process offering a service must generate a 48 bit random number which is used as the port number (capability) for that service. There are 2^{48} possible port numbers, but only a very small portion of these will be used, hence, by using a good random number generator, the probability that two of the same service numbers will be chosen is very low. This number is then made available to the authorized users of the service.

In addition to the port number, access rights are associated with each port. In this way the server process can provide different levels of access to the same object. For example, two users can have different access rights to a file if the file server allocates separate ports (one for read only, and the other for read and write) to these users.

SODS/OS

The SODS/OS is a distributed operating system designed for a local network of IBM Series/1 computers (Sincoskie and Farber, 1980). Built around the concept of communicating processes, the aim is to let a process run in one machine, have the privilege of communicating with a process on another machine, and perform I/O on peripherals on a third machine, without any knowledge that separate machines are involved. Furthermore, process migration to obtain transparent load balancing is also provided.

Processes are the active entities in SODS/OS. The medium for interprocess communication is the *'exchange'*. This is a first in, first out queue of messages which occupy a separate address space from any process (see Figure 4.14). A process wishing to send a message issues a system call requesting that the message be sent to a named exchange. The message is copied from the address space of the process into the exchange. In the same way, a process wishing to receive a message issues a system call requesting reception of a message from a named exchange.

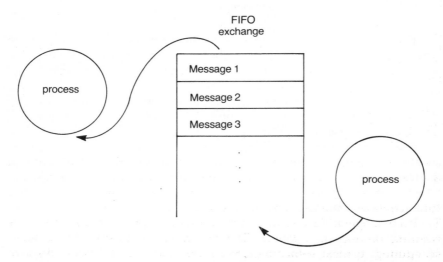

Fig. 4.14 Processes communicate via a first in, first out 'exchange', which occupies a separate address space

Access to exchanges are by way of capabilities. A process can use an exchange only if it is supplied with the capability to access that exchange. Associated with each capability are the access rights allowed to the user of the capability.

A process can issue a system call to create an exchange. The calling process also specifies the access rights it wants to the exchange. On creating the new exchange, the system returns a capability to the caller process which must then use the capability in all future reference to the exchange. A capability can be passed in a message to another process via an exchange.

A process is created in response to a 'create process' system call. The parent process provides the capability for the exchange at which the code of the child process resides – the 'code exchange', and also indicates an initial list of capabilities for the child. The system allocates space, possibly on another computer, for the new child process, copies the code from the code exchange into the allocated space and creates an appropriate context (capability table, etc.) for the child. In order to give the parent control over the child, a 'control exchange' is created and a capability for it is returned to the parent. The parent process can then send control messages – suspend, resume, etc. – to this exchange and the system will execute the appropriate operation on the child.

SODS/OS is implemented as a set of cooperating tasks which are distinct from the processes discussed above. These tasks include the process manager (PM), the exchange manager (EM), the agent, and the network manager (NM). There are two major databases in the system: one containing information on all the processes that are in the system, and the other containing information on the exchanges. Access to these databases is controlled by the PM and the EM respectively. Each machine has a PM, an EM and an NM.

When a user process issues a system call to access an exchange, an agent is activated. The agent asks the local EM to access the named exchange. If the local EM does not know that exchange, the request will be forwarded to the local NM. The local NM will determine the address of the exchange and then send the request to the remote NM. The remote NM will pass the request to its EM who gets the data and responds to the requesting agent via the same path.

The Newcastle Connection

The Newcastle Connection adds network management features to UNIX (Brownbridge et al, 1982) by superimposing a network access layer on the UNIX kernel. This layer of software lies between the kernel and the user processes (see Figure 4.15). The Newcastle Connection allows the user processes to operate as in the normal UNIX environment. At the same time, the kernel sees this new layer of software in the same way in which it sees the user processes.

It gives users, irrespective of their location, the facility to read or write files, to use any device, or to execute any command, anywhere in the network. The simple interface with the UNIX kernel, the hierarchical naming structure used in reference to files, devices and other data units, the facility to create processes and its high level language implementation are cited as some of the features in UNIX that permit extension to a distributed system.

At each host, the Newcastle Connection performs the following functions. It detects the system calls which require access to another UNIX system and forwards them accordingly, through a remote procedure call mechanism. It provides server processes in order to handle the system

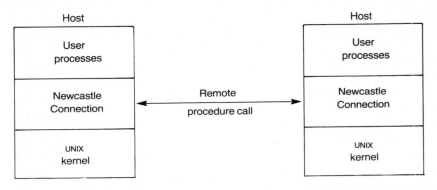

Fig. 4.15　The Newcastle Connection superimposes a network access layer over the UNIX kernel

calls coming in from remote systems. It maintains relevant parts of the global naming structure of the system in order to match referenced names with addresses. It does the mapping of file names from local to remote form, and ensures correct mapping onto its local objects. It handles communication errors as standard exceptions.

LOCUS

LOCUS is a distributed operating system that is closely related to UNIX. In fact, the kernel is designed to permit distributed operation that is upwardly compatible with UNIX (see Figure 4.16). A remote process can be created in the same way as a local one; access to a remote resource and a local resource takes the same form, and there is dynamic migration of files and programs, hence LOCUS provides a high degree of *network transparency* (Walker et al, 1983).

The standard UNIX call 'fork' is used to create a process. A process can be executed at any site in the network. The location at which the process is executed is determined from the site information provided in the process environment. Interprocess communication is supported by letting the UNIX functions 'signal' and 'pipe' operate across the network.

System service is obtained by executing system calls. Application programs and users do not know whether the system calls which they make will require access to a remote site or not. When access to a remote site is necessary, the system sends a message across the network to the remote site and then awaits the response. This is an example of a remote procedure call mechanism.

The file system uses a single tree structured naming hierarchy which covers all objects in the file system on all machines. These file names are fully transparent, i.e. the name bears no apparent relationship with the location of the file. LOCUS allows copies of files to be held at different

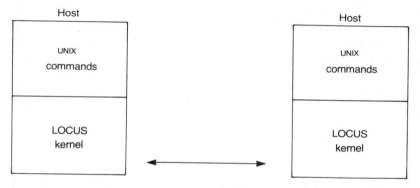

Fig. 4.16   The LOCUS distributed operating system is upward compatible with UNIX

locations and accepts the responsibility for keeping all copies up to date. Although this means additional complexities in order to maintain consistent files, the increased levels of availability can produce tremendous gains in performance. Storing multiple copies of system data structures such as file directories is viewed as essential.

Every site in the network can handle all aspects of file activity. One file operation can involve more than one site. LOCUS associates the three logical functions in a file access with three logical sites. These sites are:

(a) 'using site' (US), which issues the open file request and to which pages of the file are supplied;
(b) 'storage site' (SS), which stores the copy of the file to which the using site is given access; and
(c) 'current synchronization site' (CSS), which synchronizes the global accesses and selects storage sites to meet the open requests.

Let us briefly examine the operation of reading a file in LOCUS. The read file operation begins with an 'open' system call which specifies the filename and that the file is to be opened for reading. Directory interrogation is done in order to map the filename onto the unique directory entry. This may involve access to remote sites which hold parts of the hierarchical directory system. The CSS is interrogated next. It controls all access to the files in order to ensure that inconsistent states do not develop due to the concurrent operations.

The CSS may be the same site as the US, in which case, only a procedure call is required. If the CSS is a foreign site, the request has to be passed on via a message through the network. The CSS also selects a storage site for the read operation. The CSS knows the latest version of the file and it sends out this information to the possible sites, so that they can determine whether they have the latest version. If so, they should indicate willingness to serve as the SS.

The CSS may hold the latest version of the file. If this is the case, it can select itself to serve as the SS. The US can also be the one storing the latest version. In anticipation of this, the US includes an indication of the version of the file that it stores in its initial message to the CSS. The CSS can then ascertain if this is the latest version and select the US as the SS. The read operations can begin after the US receives a response to its 'open' request from the CSS.

Software and hardware malfunction can cause one part of the network to be isolated from another part. This is referred to as *partitioning* of the network. It constitutes a serious threat to the integrity of a file which has copies in separate partitions. One step that can be taken is to restrict use of a file to a single partition. However, since this reduces the availability of the file, LOCUS allows updates to proceed in each partition. When the partitions are subsequently merged, LOCUS attempts to resolve any conflicts due to the separate updates. We will return to this problem of partition failures in Chapter 6.

LOCUS provides dynamic reconfiguration of the network. Should some part of the system fail, LOCUS attempts to allocate alternative resources without the user being aware that a failure has occurred. This facility is possible because of the extent of replication of resources. For example, if a site fails it is possible that copies of the files being accessed there may be available elsewhere.

4.2.5 Comparison of examples

In our examples, we looked at two distributed kernels – Accent and the V kernel, two altogether new distributed operating systems – Amoeba and SODS/OS and two projects that are extensions of UNIX – the Newcastle Connection, and LOCUS.

In interprocess communication, we saw remote procedure call and message passing. The Newcastle Connection and LOCUS both use RPC, thus placing confidence in the well-known procedure call environment. Accent and SODS/OS use message passing without automatic blocking. Each of these systems provides a data structure outside of the communicating processes for handling the messages. Although they are named differently – *port* and *exchange* – they are fundamentally alike.

Ports and exchanges are both created on the request of processes, controlled by the operating system, and can have queues of messages. Access control is capability-based, and access rights can be passed via messages to other processes.

The V kernel and Amoeba also use message passing but with blocking on sender for a reply. Thus the protocol behaves somewhat like RPC. Messages in Amoeba are sent to and received from ports in a capability-based protection scheme. Processes in the V kernel are uniquely named and this name is used as the destination address in the messages.

Accent, the V kernel and Amoeba all support a client-server relationship for sharing of resources. A service can be accessed as long as it is available and known by the client. SODS/OS provides a similar arrangement by allowing processes owning resources to receive messages on a first in, first out exchange. LOCUS, on the other hand, has distributed control of multiple copies of objects, e.g. multiple version files. In this regard, LOCUS has some of the characteristics of a distributed database system and is, therefore, more complex than the other systems. The Newcastle Connection uses the resource management features of UNIX.

4.3 OPERATING SYSTEMS FOR PARALLEL COMPUTING

We will look briefly at three approaches to operating system design for parallel computing. They are the *master-slave system*, the *floating supervisor control* and the *distributed operating system* configuration.

Master-slave organization

In a master-slave organization, only one processor, the master, executes the operating system. This simplifies the operating system design, since the control of all system tables is centralized. The other processors operate in a slave mode – they obey the master's commands. They are scheduled work and must make requests of the master to execute supervisory functions on their behalf.

In this arrangement, any failure in the master is a failure of the system. One example system is the DEC System-10 – a two processor configuration. This master-slave mode of operation is suitable in a system where the work load is well defined, and in asymmetrical systems where the slaves have less functional capability than the master, as is the case in associative processors, systolic arrays and SIMD systems (see Chapter 2).

The efficient use of the parallelism available in parallel systems like SIMD machines must be one of the goals of the operating system. The operating system must be able to recognize the parallel streams in the user programs and make the necessary allocations to the PEs. The user should be able to easily identify and specify the parallel activity in the application being programmed. Adequate software tools are necessary in order to facilitate this identification and specification. We will look at these issues in Chapter 7.

Floating supervisor control

In this scheme, all the processors and other resources are treated symmetrically (Hwang and Briggs, 1984). All the processors execute the operating system, and the supervisory role floats from processor to processor. Furthermore, several of the processors can execute some supervisory service routines simultaneously. Examples of this mode of operation are DEC's symmetrical multiprocessing (SMP) system and the Hydra on the C.mmp.

Some of the advantages of this system over an asymmetric one are better load balancing, improved fault tolerance and increased availability of resources. However, particular attention must be paid to the contention that can arise owing to the considerable degree of shared system code and tables.

The distributed operating system

This scheme is called the distributed operating system configuration because it fits the description of the distributed operating system in the network environment. It is one operating system running in an MIMD machine with each processor-memory node containing a separate copy of the operating system kernel.

One example system is the Cosmic Cube (Seitz, 1985) which was introduced in Chapter 2. The basic unit of computation is the process – a sequential program that sends and receives messages. Each node may contain many processes which execute concurrently. The kernel at each node can spawn, schedule and kill processes, as well as manage storage and error conditions. Interprocess communication is via a message passing scheme. The kernel handles the queuing and routing of the messages on behalf of the processes at its node, as well as the messages that are passing through on their way to a remote node.

The availability of programming languages that allow relatively easy representation of parallelism can be a considerable aid to the operating system designer. We will examine such language projects in Chapter 7.

4.4 SUMMARY

Operating systems for computer networks can be divided into two classes. These are:

(a) network operating systems; and
(b) distributed operating systems.

The network operating system allows the running of heterogeneous operating systems at local hosts and ties these together by a system of agent processes. The distributed approach replaces the heterogeneous systems by a single network-wide operating system.

A key issue in the design of these systems is the level of transparency. It seems that a high level of transparency is a desirable goal. Users should not be bothered with a number of network details before they can benefit from the services offered. However, as the level of transparency increases so does the level of complexity in the operating system design.

The form of interprocess communication is a distinguishing feature in the design of distributed operating systems. Two common alternative schemes are:

(a) remote procedure call; and
(b) message passing.

One approach to the design of a distributed operating system is to add network facilities to a traditional, multiprogramming operating system. Another approach is to build an entirely new system.

Some other issues are:

(a) where to site the agent process in the network operating system;
(b) what system will be used to manage the resources; and
(c) what are the network standards that are being followed.

A parallel computer system needs an operating system that is designed specifically to exercise the parallel hardware features and at the same time create a comfortable working environment for the user. Three categories into which operating systems for parallel computing can be divided are:

(a) master-slave organization;
(b) floating supervisor control; and
(c) a distributed operating system configuration.

4.5 QUESTIONS

4.1 Distinguish between a network operating system and a distributed operating system.

4.2 Why are distributed operating systems more common in local area networks than in wide area networks?

4.3 Indicate the functions of the agent process in a network operating system.

4.4 What does the term network transparency mean? Why is it a desirable feature in operating systems for networks?

4.5 How can the system provide network transparency at the user command level?

4.6 Discuss the alternatives available for the siting of an agent process.

4.7 Distinguish between procedure call and message passing as interprocess communication schemes.

4.8 What is a capability-based protection scheme?

4.9 LOCUS permits updates to continue on copies of the same file in separate partitions after some network failure. Can you suggest a system for bringing all the copies of the file to a consistent state after the network resumes full operation?

4.10 What is the relationship between the network protocols as discussed in Chapter 3 and operating systems as discussed in this chapter?

4.11 Given that the agent process is implemented as a user process at each host computer, how can concurrent access to network facilities from several processes at the same host computer be supported?

4.12 Indicate differences in implementation between entry to an agent via an explicit command (external to program code) and entry via a statement within an object module.

4.13 If the agent process is a user process in a virtual memory management environment with paging, suggest alternative policies that you would adopt with respect to the removal of the pages occupied by the agent. Provide advantages and disadvantages.

4.6 REFERENCES

1 Ball, J.E. et al, 1979. 'Perspectives on message-based distributed computing', *Proceedings, Computer Networking Symposium*, Gaithersburg, Maryland IEEE, 46–51.

2 Birrell, A.D. and Nelson, B.J., 1984. 'Implementing Remote Procedure Calls', *ACM Transactions on Computer Systems*, **2**, 1 (Feb.), 39–59.

3 Brownbridge, D.R., Marshall, L.F. and Randell, B., 1982. 'The Newcastle Connection or UNIXes of the World Unite!', *Software Practice and Experience*, **12**, 12, 1147–1162.

4 Cheriton, D.R., 1984. 'The V kernel: A software base for distributed systems', *IEEE Software*, **1** (Apr.), 19–42.

5 Collinson, R.P.A., 1984. *Operating Systems Interfaces to LANs*. Lecture notes for

Cambridge Ring LAN course at Computing Laboratory, University of Kent at Canterbury, Kent, England.

6 Donnelley, J., 1980. 'Components of a network operating system' in *A pragmatic view of Distributed Processing Systems*, 253–273, ed. K.J. Thurber, IEEE Computer Society.

7 Hwang, K. and Briggs, F.A., 1984. *Computer Architecture and Parallel Processing*, New York, McGraw-Hill.

8 Jones, A.K. et al, 1979. 'STAROS: A multiprocessor operating system for the Support of Task Forces', *Proceedings of the Seventh Symposium on Operating Systems Principles*, ACM, Pacific Grove, California, 117–127.

9 Rashid, R.F. and Robertson, G.G., 1981. 'Accent: A communication oriented network operating system kernel', *Proceedings of the Eighth Symposium on Operating Systems Principles*, ACM, Pacific Grove, California, **15**, 5, 64–75.

10 Seitz, C.L., 1985. 'The Cosmic Cube', *Communications of the ACM*, **28**, 1(Jan), 22–33.

11 Sincoskie, W.D. and Farber, D.J., 1980. 'SODS/OS: A Distributed Operating System for the IBM Series/1', *ACM SIGOPS, Operating Systems Review*, **14**, 3(Jul), 46–54.

12 Tanenbaum, A.S., 1981. *Computer Networks*, Englewood Cliffs: Prentice Hall Inc.

13 Tanenbaum, A.S. and Mullender, S., 1981. 'An overview of the Amoeba distributed operating system', *ACM SIGOPS, Operating Systems Review*, **15**, 3, 51–64.

14 Tanenbaum, A.S. and Van Renesse, R., 1985. 'Distributed Operating Systems', *ACM Computing Surveys*, **17**, 4(Dec), 419–470.

15 Walker, B. et al, 1983. 'The LOCUS distributed operating system', *Proceedings of the Ninth ACM Symposium on Operating Systems Principles*, Bretton Woods, New Hampshire, **17**, 5, 49–70.

16 Wilkes, M. and Needham, R., 1979. *The Cambridge CAP Computer and its Operating System*, Rotterdam: North Holland.

17 Wulf, W., et al, 1974. 'HYDRA: The kernel of a Multiprocessor Operating System', *Communications of the ACM*, **17**, 6, 337–345.

CHAPTER FIVE

SERVERS IN THE CLIENT-SERVER NETWORK MODEL

Computer networks provide a good opportunity for sharing expensive resources. Although hardware components are showing a rapid decrease in cost, one can still show that the price/performance ratios, in many instances, favor the sharing of such units. Large capacity direct access disks can be shared among the stations on a local area network, as can special purpose equipment like the latest technology e.g. laser printers and graph plotters. In some local environments such as schools, it is the usual practice to share one floppy disk drive and an inexpensive printer among several microcomputers on a LAN.

Sharing these devices involves a great deal more than just physically attaching them to a communications network. Software has to be designed and written in order to manage these units effectively. This software has to deal both with the characteristics of the network to which the units are attached and the particular units which are to be shared.

In Chapter 4, the design of network operating systems and distributed operating systems was discussed. These operating systems facilitate the sharing of network resources. Network operating systems allow host stations to run their own operating systems. To each operating system is added the facility to accommodate network-access commands. These commands may possess a local identity and can, therefore, differ from the host computer. For example, the command name for loading a file from a disk (wherever that disk is located) may be 'load' on one operating system, while it may be '*load' on another.

Distributed operating systems aim to establish a uniform interface between the network and the user, irrespective of where that user is

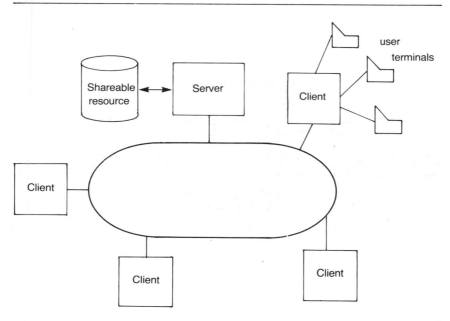

Fig. 5.1 Server manages a shareable resource used by a number of clients in the network. The users log on to the client machines

located. In such an environment, there is one homogeneous operating system. As the user moves from station to station, there is no need for that user to learn a new set of commands.

An additional software tool used to provide shared resources on the network is the *server*. The server is an integral part of the client-server model of distributed computing discussed in Chapter 2. Servers can be used in network and distributed operating system environments. In fact, the client-server model can be used as a basis for building a distributed operating system.

The server can be viewed as a piece of software that manages a shareable resource. Usually the resource resides at one location in the network and the server is run on the computer at which the resource resides. The server must offer an acceptable level of service to all the users of the network. The mechanics of accessing this server are hidden from the network user by interface software which resides at the separate stations. This interface is usually referred to as the *client* (see Figure 5.1).

Some server systems have been designed to manage similar resources at multiple sites. For example, recall the discussion of the LOCUS distributed operating system in Chapter 4, where it was observed that copies of files can be held at several different locations in the network. The client has no knowledge of which location is being accessed. This property of the distributed system is called *location transparency*.

Easily the most common, and certainly one of the first, server applications in the network environment is the *file server*. The need to store and retrieve large volumes of data is widespread. One of the greatest appeals of computerization is the ability to cope with the vast data storage and retrieval needs that exist almost everywhere. Hence techniques to offer such a facility at minimum cost and acceptable speed have to be developed and continually maintained. The file server is one of these techniques. In addition to the usual file management functions performed by filing systems, the file server must cater for the problems introduced by network access.

Other services can be provided for network users by using a server system. Three that are relatively common are the **printer server**, the **name server** and the **mail server**. In the following sections, the file, name, printer and mail servers will be discussed. Many of the issues highlighted here are applicable to other server systems.

5.1 FILE SERVERS

A fundamental objective of a file server system is to provide secondary storage on a large capacity, high performance disk for files accessible by clients spread over the network. This storage will be referred to as the *file-store*. Levels of service which can extend to a full-scale filing system can be built upon this basic facility (Svobodova, 1984). In the sections which follow we will look at:

(a) how the type of service provided can vary;
(b) some different forms that the organization of the server can take;
(c) relevant aspects of communication protocols; and
(d) mechanisms that are employed in order to ensure the security and integrity of the data stored.

5.1.1 Type of service

The users of a file system should be able to create, read, write and delete files. In addition, they should enjoy some level of privacy and security and maybe even the privilege of sharing files with other users. Furthermore, the users will be concerned about aspects of performance of the system such as response times and frequency of breakdowns.

Traditionally, all of these facilities were implemented at a local site and there still are many advantages in this approach. Such an implementation gave more control and hence more physical security and more resilience to failures. However, the user had to be satisfied with what was available locally. The file server and the network have changed this. Now there is the question of how to make the best use of local and remote resources.

One way to provide service when all the files are held at a remote location is to allow only file transfer activity. Irrespective of whether the user wishes to use the entire file or merely to read a single data item in that file, the entire file must be *down-loaded* to the client machine. All other file activity – read, write, append, etc. – is performed at the local station. The file server behaves like a repository for the storage and retrieval of files.

This is a primitive approach which contains many limitations, chief among them being the restriction of file size by the availability of storage at the client machine. Another setback is that even a small update would necessitate at least two file transfers – remote to local followed by local to remote. However, this type of service can be suitable where the files are programs which can be loaded and run on demand at different stations.

Another approach to client service would be to allow access to the file-store at a *page/block*, record or even word/byte level. Access to individual pages or blocks would mean that the client can fetch at one time some number of records determined by the block size. This can be extended to the support of *virtual memory* systems for the client machines. Access to individual records would require the server to extract the appropriate record from its block before transmission. Word or byte access allows manipulation by the client of the individual data fields of a record, which can be used to accommodate a distributed database system (see Chapter 6).

A corresponding increase in the size of data areas allocated to address resolution may come with the decrease in size of the unit of access (file, page, byte). However, with concurrent access being supported, the smaller units of access permit wider sharing and so increased availability of the resource which can generate better response times.

If the unit of access is a file then it may be necessary to let only one user access that file at a time unless multiple copies are stored, in which case there can be simultaneous access but to separate copies. If the unit of access is a part of the file, e.g. a page, then it is possible to allow parallel access to the file where each user has a separate page. Of course, it must not be forgotten that the entire file may be less than a page. However, there will be greater demands on the file server system for adequate concurrency control mechanisms to prevent deadlocks and avoid corruption of file contents.

Another aspect of service is the provision of backup and recovery measures. The file server may assume the responsibility to safeguard the user's files against failures. This would require automatic backup of files or their components in order to facilitate recovery from system malfunction. We will look at this in section 5.1.4.

5.1.2 Organization

The type of service provided by a file server would affect the organization of the file server itself and the specification of the client software. The

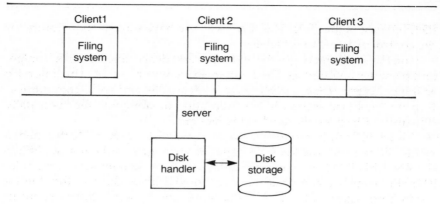

Fig. 5.2 Client-server environment with each client creating its own filing
system

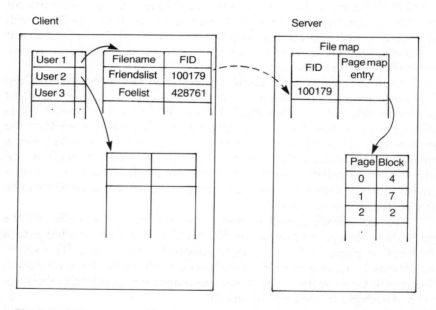

Fig. 5.3 Client maintains filing system to map local textual names onto global
FIDs

question of organization must also extend to the distribution of functions
between the file server and clients.

An acceptable framework for a file server system is that of a number of
clients, each with its own filing system, superimposed upon the file
storage/retrieval facilities offered by the server (see Figure 5.2). In this
organization, the client will have a directory system to allow the correspondence between the users' textual file names and the global unique file

ID (FID) (see Figure 5.3). The client will also have some responsibility for the control of access to these files.

The file server manages the allocation and deallocation of disk storage, and provides an interface for client-server communication. This interface will include *primitive* commands (e.g. create file) and some communication protocol (see section 5.1.3). Allocation of storage to files is usually dynamic with space allocated as the files grow.

Global file naming is done at the server level. In response to the client's create file request, the file server allocates storage and the unique FID to the file. This FID is given to the client for all future reference to that file. The client must ensure that only authorized users can use this file by controlling access to the FID. If the server allows access to any client in possession of the FID, a client can send the FID of a file to another client, thus permitting access from different machines.

One problem that can arise is that of the undeletable file. This can occur if a file can be deleted only after an explicit request from the client and, due to some malfunction, the client fails to record the FID of a file that was created by the server. Techniques to avoid this problem will be seen as we continue through the following sections.

If the file server provides automatic backup and recovery facilities then it may be necessary to categorize files. For example, files can be classified as recoverable, robust or ordinary (Svobodova, 1984). A *recoverable* file is one for which there always exists an earlier consistent state to which the system can revert when an operation on the file fails. A *robust* file is guaranteed to survive failures of the storage device and medium. An *ordinary* file is given no special treatment. Redundancy in the storage of files or parts of a file forms the basis upon which these special files can be supported (see section 5.1.4).

Files are usually stored in noncontiguous fixed-size blocks on the secondary storage medium. The file itself is therefore divided into a number of pages and each page is mapped onto a block. The server maintains a *page map* to point to the blocks in which the pages are stored. There will be an entry in the server's root directory pointing to the page map of each file stored (see Figure 5.3).

In addition to storing the data contents of a file, one must store certain attributes of that file. These attributes – file creation time, file length, the time when last modified, etc. – will form the file header and this file header can be stored with the page map. Therefore, access to the header will not necessitate traveling all the way to the actual data blocks.

The unit of access available to the client will determine how much data are stored for mapping the client's logical request onto the physical address. If only file transfer is permitted, then, on the initial request, the server will retrieve the entire file via the page map. If the unit of access is some part of the file, the server must employ some additional procedure to extract the required subrange.

The specification of such a subrange is based upon the client's view of a file at the server level. One approach is to let the client see all files as a fixed-length, contiguous string of bytes or words. The client may then be permitted to access any contiguous substring of words/bytes. The server does the mapping onto the physical storage blocks.

For example, a request to read a sequence of bytes may take the following form:

read-data(FID, no-of-bytes, first-byte-no).

The server must execute some algorithm to find the page or pages which contain these bytes. As an exercise, you should be able to provide an algorithm to locate the pages and then follow the page map to obtain the appropriate blocks or disk sectors.

The client, on the other hand, may be allowed to divide the file into pages and specify subrange requests within page boundaries. However, different clients may find different page sizes suitable which presents a problem to the server, and an arbitrary subrange within a file may be preferable. In this case, the paging will be transparent to the client.

The FID can be designed to contain information on the storage address of the file. This means that the *root of the file* (i.e. the location of header and page map) cannot move and therefore must be updated in place. Alternatively, the FID may be completely independent of the location of the file, in which case the additional mapping mechanism is necessary to locate the root when given the FID.

Another form that the relationship between the clients and the server can take is to let the server maintain one global filing system which all the clients must use (see Figure 5.4). In this arrangement, the client does not

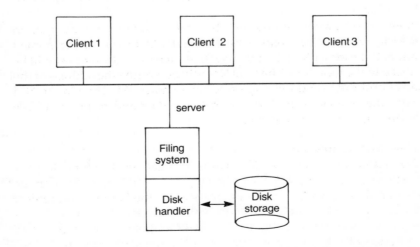

Fig. 5.4   All clients use the same filing system which is provided by the server

maintain a local file system. All file commands are channeled to the file server. This approach has been adopted by many small microcomputer LANs.

5.1.3 Communication protocols

In Chapter 3 we looked at the ISO reference model and identified several of the important issues of protocol which arise at each of the layers of the architecture. Most of those issues are relevant here. In particular, the aim is reliable communication in the face of unavoidable transmission errors and other system failures.

Many networks do not conform exactly with the ISO model. However, there will be protocols similar to the data link and network layer protocols upon which the file server can establish a transport service that it considers suitable. Whether or not the network provides a datagram or virtual circuit service is particularly important. If it is datagram, the file server protocol must handle the packet reassembly in order to preserve the correct sequence on the data transmitted. This will arise since the messages transferred between server and client will often require more than a single datagram packet, and therefore the multiple packets can arrive out of sequence.

Other matters that would be of concern in the server system are:

(a) *flow control* – one must ensure that neither the server nor the client is saturated;
(b) *duplicate requests* – an expected response is not received and, on assuming in error that the request was lost, a duplicate is sent; and
(c) *a nonresponding client* – a client failing in the middle of a transaction.

Two examples of protocol models used are:

(a) a **three-message protocol** (Mitchell, 1982) in which the client makes a request, the server responds and then the client acknowledges receipt of the response; and
(b) the **single-shot protocol** in which only repeatable requests are used (Needham and Herbert, 1982).

In the three-message protocol, the server can throw away the data for a response once it has received the acknowledgment of receipt from the client; and the server can repeat the response if the client duplicates the request. However, the act of repeating the response does not mean that the activity requested has been repeated. In fact, this can corrupt data areas, e.g. imagine the result of performing an 'append' more times than the required single operation. Hence the server must be able to detect the duplicate request. A common solution is to number requests sequentially, therefore the duplicate will contain the same number as the original.

In the single-shot protocol all requests should generate actions which, when repeated, have the same effect. Such requests are sometimes referred to as *idempotent*. For example, read or write is repeatable, but append is not. It would seem from this that an append can never be allowed. However, this is not the case. Additions can be handled within the context of a set length of the file. The client specifies this set number of bytes before additions are requested. The subsequent append request must not result in this set length being exceeded.

This means that the client interface must be designed so that all requests are repeatable. A simple timer expiry can control the request/ response activity. The timer starts when the request is sent. If the timer expires before the response is received, the request is repeated. If many messages are lost or delayed, the number of repetitions can be high, hence such a protocol should operate in a highly reliable network.

5.1.4 Security and integrity

Security and integrity problems in a filing system are compounded by network access. Files must be protected from unauthorized access at local as well as remote sites. Concurrent access by multiple users can leave files in incorrect states thus affecting the integrity of the data stored. Stations participating in transactions can fail in the middle of the exercise generating inconsistent states across the network.

First of all, what can be regarded as a transaction must be agreed upon. A user may request that some single operation be performed on a file, e.g. open file, or read file, etc. However, the user may like to perform a sequence of operations, e.g. open file, read file, write file, and close file. In the second case, there are multiple accesses forming a composite set of operations to the same file. During the processing of these operations it will be necessary to prevent access by any other user in order to avoid corruption of the stored information. We will regard both the single operation and the composite sequence as a transaction. The client interface must include primitives for indicating the beginning and the end of a transaction.

Concurrency control techniques have to be implemented in order to serialize the transactions wherever problems can arise (see Chapter 6). Locking of the areas accessed has proven to be quite an adequate measure. However, there are always questions relating to the length of time that locks are held and the extent of the data areas that are locked. In addition, there are the problems of *indefinite postponement* and deadlocks that can arise when resources can be locked away.

The *two-phase lock* protocol has been adopted in many instances to control concurrent transactions. A transaction must acquire locks on the data areas to be accessed in the first phase (see section 6.4.2). In the second phase, the locks are released. Having released a lock, a transaction cannot obtain a lock on the same or any other data item. Provision must be made to prevent, avoid or detect deadlocks. This may involve having to break locks and abort clients' transactions in order to put the system back into production (Mitchell, 1982).

Name and password authentication at begin-transaction time can be done to ensure only authorized access. Access control lists will have to be maintained in order to perform the necessary checking. Capability-based techniques may also be employed to control access. In the Cambridge File Server (Needham and Herbert, 1982) all files are regarded as objects and, in order to refer to a file, one must possess the capability. These capabilities are unique across the filing system and (hopefully) cannot be guessed by an intruder.

Software and hardware failures are a serious threat to the integrity of filing systems. What is the state of a file in the event of such a failure during a file update? This problem is more severe when concurrent access to large databases is allowed (see Chapter 6). Some steps that can be taken involve making copies of critical material on separate physical volumes, and separating directory or indexing information from actual data.

An additional technique is the use of *atomic transactions* (Lampson, 1981; Sturgis et al, 1980). An atomic transaction either occurs successfully or has no effect. Any transaction which includes a change (an update) to any data item must be so handled that, should it not complete successfully, the change must be undone. Hence the system must maintain recoverable files.

The aim is to avoid overwriting the actual data in secondary storage. The use of a *shadow-page* technique is common among designers. Before updating a page of the file, a free disk block/sector is obtained from the block allocation map. This block will be used to store the updated page. The page map of the file is appropriately modified to point to this new page in addition to maintaining the pointer to the old page. Furthermore, an *intentions log* may be used to record all these steps (see Figure 5.5).

There seems to be some disagreement with respect to which page is actually the shadow. Svobodova (1984) called the *new* pages the shadows, while Brown, et al (1985) called the *old* pages the shadows. The labeling seems to depend on the page to which read access is allowed before the update is *committed*. We shall call the old page the shadow.

A transaction has reached its *commit point* (or it can be committed) when any subsequent crash at the server will not prevent the transaction from completing successfully. The commit point is, therefore, the point at which all changes to the client's data can be made permanent.

With the shadow-page technique, the transaction is committed when the new pages are completely updated, and the relevant entries have been made in the intentions log. During the update, the page exists in two versions: the shadow page and the new page. When it is safe to make the change permanent, the file map is atomically updated to point to the updated page only. The space occupied by the shadow is therefore freed.

File directory

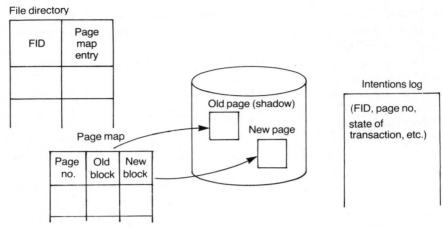

Fig. 5.5 Atomic transactions using shadow-page technique

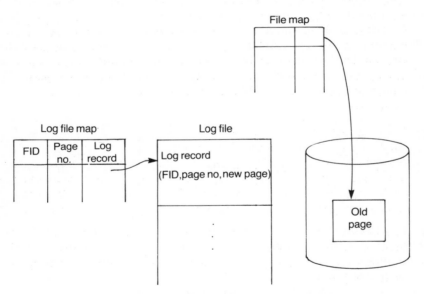

Fig. 5.6 Atomic transactions using a logging technique

An alternative technique for recoverable files is the use of an *undo/redo log*. This technique involves appending a log record to a *log file* and making an entry in a log file map (see Figure 5.6). The log record may contain transaction ID, the pair (FID, page number) of the page being updated and the actual data contents of the page. The entry in the log file map associates the pair (FID, page number) with the appropriate record in the log file.

Brown et al (1985) have given five advantages that the log mechanism has over the shadow-page technique. These are:

(a) The total cost of I/Os performed in the log technique is often less than that when using shadow pages. The excess cost arises in the shadow-page technique because:

    (i) it has to update the file map and the free block/sector allocation map recoverably;

    (ii) every read and write in the shadow-page technique is random, while the log technique does sequential writing and buffered reading which is less costly;

    (iii) every transaction in the shadow page requires an update of the file map while the log updates the map only when the number of pages is altered.

Since the pages updated by a transaction are not always clustered into one page of the file map, the file map update can be very costly.

(b) The log technique supports sequential file organization on the disk where logically sequential pages are stored in a physically sequential manner. This improves the performance for sequential processing as well as random accesses. Random access is improved because the file map for the physically sequential file is smaller than for the non-sequential. The file map entries in the sequential case can point to longer physical extents. In the nonsequential file it is necessary to enter individual page addresses. Hence the shadow-page technique is more costly.

(c) The logging technique can defer more work until after commit than the shadow page. Whereas the shadow page involves a write to the file pages before commit, the log does this *after* commit, hence responses in the log technique can be quicker. Furthermore, the implementation of the logging system may accommodate a stream of updates to the same file page before forcing the write to the appropriate disk sector.

(d) File back-up is easier to implement in the log-based system. This involves two-copy logging and periodic file system dumps. With the shadow-page technique it may be necessary to introduce a logging system to provide back-up.

(e) The logging system can be superimposed on an existing file system. There is no requirement for any special features in the implementation, since the log technique involves merely reading and writing files. Hence the implementation is less involved than for the shadow-page system.

5.1.5 Examples of file servers

XDFS (Xerox Distributed File System)
XDFS was designed at Xerox Palo Alto Research Center (PARC) to support database-oriented applications (Mitchell, 1982), and the first version

became operational in 1977. The unit of data access is a page subrange, therefore read-data and write-data requests can specify a range of bytes within a single page.

The directory subsystem is implemented as a client of the file server. A file is created at the server and an FID is returned in response to a client's request which must be made after a transaction has been opened. Multiple versions of a file are supported. Files in XDFS are divided into pages which are mapped onto noncontiguous storage blocks. Mapping information is held in a common map that associates the pair (FID, page number) with the address of the storage block. The FID of the file contains the ID of the disk volume on which the file is stored.

The underlying network layer protocol in XDFS is *Pup* (PARC universal packet) datagram service which can transport a packet of at most 512 data bytes. Upon this is built the three-message protocol: send-request, receive-response, send-acknowledgment.

Access control is identity-based and handled by the directory service at the client. Concurrency control is managed automatically by the server. A two-phase locking protocol is used. Read-data and write-data requests set locks and these locks are released by explicit end and abort transaction operations.

XDFS allows three types of locks: read, intention-write and commit. The intention-write lock allows a transaction to modify its own copy of the file. This is a 'soft' write lock which lets readers access other copies of the file while the lock is on. The intention-write lock must be changed to a commit lock, i.e. a 'hard' write lock at commit time. The transaction then has exclusive access to the file. Locks are time-limited thus giving the system the freedom to break locks in order to avoid deadlocks.

XDFS supports atomic transactions and these transactions can include multiple files in multiple servers, hence XDFS can be viewed as a fully distributed system. The server to which the client sends the 'begin transaction' request will act as the transaction coordinator. Furthermore several clients can participate in a transaction. Shadow pages and an intentions log are used to implement atomic transactions.

CFS (Cambridge file server)

CFS was developed at Cambridge University to support, as clients, general-purpose operating systems (Needham and Herbert, 1982) and has been operational since 1980. In CFS, the unit of data access is an arbitrary subrange of a file, therefore read and write requests can specify a sequential range of bytes within a file.

CFS maintains two types of objects: an index and a file. The index is used to construct directories of a filing system. There is a root index known only by the server. A new user must obtain from a system administrator an index which will form the root of that user's directory. The system administrator creates this new index, stores its ID in the system's root

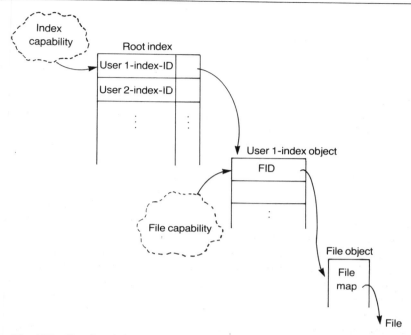

Fig. 5.7 The Cambridge File Server maintains index objects for constructing user directories which point to file objects

index, and then gives the ID to the user. The ID is the capability to the index (see Figure 5.7).

Now that the index exists and is known, a client can specify that a file be created. The server will record its FID in the specified index. Since the FID is placed in an index, the 'undeletable file' problem does not arise. A file is deleted automatically when its FID is not in an index reachable from the root index. CFS has a 'garbage collector' that reclaims all space allocated to objects that cannot be reached from the root index.

CFS stores files as a multilevel tree of fixed-size blocks. The actual data are stored in 2K blocks and the page maps are stored in 512-byte blocks. The FID of the file contains the address of the file root which means that the root cannot move.

CFS runs on a Cambridge ring which provides a very reliable datagram service. It uses a send-request, receive-response protocol with all operations being repeatable. Access control in CFS is capability based where the IDs of the objects (index, file) are the capabilities. The FID of the file is divided into two fields: the disk address of the file root and a random number. The probability of guessing the correct combination of disk address and random number is low, thus the capability is very difficult to forge.

With respect to concurrency control, CFS gives exclusive access to a single writer or shared access to multiple readers. There is no additional deadlock control mechanism. CFS supports atomic transactions on single files only. It uses shadow pages and an intentions log in its maintenance of recoverable files.

Swallow

Swallow was designed in 1980 at the Massachusetts Institute of Technology as a distributed data storage system providing atomic transactions on multiple files and multiple servers. At the time of Svobodova's survey (Svobodova, 1984) it was not fully implemented.

The unit of data access in Swallow is a file which is classified as an object. Although the interface transfers only files, these objects can be very small. Files are represented as multilevel trees of variable-size blocks. Several versions of a file are kept in a *linked list* with the file header being held as a separate structure pointing to the latest version. The FID of the file does not contain storage address information; a table is used to map the FID to the address of the file header.

Swallow uses capabilities and encryption for access control. File versions are stored and transferred in encrypted form. The client must know the encryption key to understand the contents. It also needs a write capability to update a file and the data used in the update must be encrypted by the client. In addition, for each transaction, a separate capability is needed to be able to commit that transaction.

Since Swallow stores multiple versions of a file, concurrent reads can access older versions while a new version is being committed. It uses timestamps in concurrency control in order to serialize transactions that can generate inconsistent states.

Atomic transactions are handled by the creation of tentative versions. Write-data requests cause a tentative version of the whole file to be created. If the transaction fails, the tentative version will be ignored.

Swallow establishes a virtual circuit to transmit data when the number of bytes exceeds the packet size of the underlying network. The receiver acknowledges at the end of the file transfer indicating any missing packets. The sender resends only the missing packets. This process is repeated until all the packets are received.

5.2   NAME SERVERS

5.2.1   General discussion

All the services provided on a network must be identifiable by some name. In order to make these services widely available, not only must the name be known but also the specific address. In fact, the name must be mapped onto an address which should include both a host or station identity and a port number. The port number will distinguish it from other services offered at the same station/host.

One approach is to require that all clients of a service must possess the address of that service. This means storing as many copies of that address as there are clients. The result is some inflexibility of the system to machine and service mobility. The addition of a new service also means making the address known to all the users.

The use of a name server removes these constraints. All users are allowed to refer to services by some symbolic name. The name server maintains look up information to perform the translation from names to addresses. It is necessary that clients know the address only of the name server which will perform the name-to-address transformation.

In addition, the name server may be designed to answer requests for the name of a service given the address of that service. This is particularly useful for monitoring purposes.

The performance of the network is, however, tied to the name server. Special measures must be taken to ensure the reliability of the name server. Table entries for critical services may be held in nonvolatile primary store to facilitate fast recovery after power failures. The hardware components should be robust and spares readily available to make the system acceptably resilient.

5.2.2 An example

We will take a brief look at a name server that has been implemented on the Cambridge ring as part of the Cambridge Distributed Computing System at Cambridge University (Needham and Herbert, 1982). A machine has a distinct textual name as well as a unique numerical address. That address is the ring station number to which the machine is attached. A machine can host several services each of which has a unique textual name within that machine. The only address that any machine on the ring needs to know is that of the name server from which all other addresses are obtained.

The name server provides the following services:

(a) A client can ask for the location of a service by quoting the name of the service. If the service is provided by more than one machine, the name of the service must also include a textual machine name component, e.g. 'GIVEFILE-BRAVO' is the name of the 'GIVEFILE' service on the machine 'BRAVO'. The location of the service includes a machine number, a port number and, in some cases, a function code that may distinguish between the services offered at a particular port.

(b) There is a 'who am I?' service which allows a machine to obtain its textual name.

(c) A client can ask for the name of any machine on the ring by giving the address of the ring station.

The single shot protocol described in section 5.1.3 is used in these interactions.

The name server contains an initial table in ROM to enable system restarts, but the whole name table is kept on the file server. The presence of an entry in the name table is no indication that the service is actually running, it merely states where the service will run when it is available.

Any alteration to the names of services can be requested only by the machines that provide the services. There are two name server operations available for this: *add name* and *delete name*. An up-to-date printed list of all the services and their locations can be generated by any machine.

The name server is the most fundamental of all the services in the Cambridge System. Its failure will bring the system to a halt. However the small, simple machine used in the system has proved to be sufficiently reliable.

5.3 PRINTER SERVERS

5.3.1 General discussion

High-quality printing services are still relatively expensive. There is an increasing level of work being done in the development of document and text preparation computer programs. Therefore, in addition to the usual demands for hard-copy computer output, there are now demands for output on sophisticated typesetting systems.

It will most probably be a very long time before these expensive devices can be allocated exclusively to individual client-machines. Moreover, in a network environment, the demand may never be so great as to require the exclusive use of a printer by one client. Some limited number (more often than not, only one) of these high-quality printers will have to be shared among the users of the network.

Clients must be able to address the printer server (possibly with the help of a name server), and send print commands and the documents that are to be printed. Some communication protocol as discussed under file servers must be used. Since a printer can service only one user at a time then the server must perform some buffer management and queuing.

Steps must be employed to provide some degree of error and flow control. Adequate measures may already exist in the lower-level protocol layers, or it may be necessary to construct additional control routines in order to ensure an acceptable level of service.

5.3.2 Two examples

(a) At the Computing laboratory, University of Kent at Canterbury (UKC) there is a project, directed by Heather Brown, to provide high quality output from various typesetting systems. Part of this project involved the use of a printer server to share these high quality facilities among users of their local area network (Utting, 1984).

A laser printing system has been attached directly to a Cambridge Ring LAN. The printer server accepts a description of a document from clients on the Cambridge Ring, transforms it into a page bit-map and passes it on to the printer.

The system includes a Canon LBP-10 laser printer, a UKC-designed 4K word FIFO plus the logic necessary to convert 16-bit parallel data to 1.8 MHz bit-serial data, a 1 Mbyte Motorola 68000-based system from Orbis of Cambridge which includes a Motorola 6809-based Cambridge Ring interface handling the Basic Block Protocol.

In order to print a document, a client uses a Document Transmission Format (DTF) to transmit a description of the document to the server. The server is used mainly by UNIX systems which support T_EX and TROFF document preparation tools. The client must map its requirements onto the DTF for handling by the server.

(b) Acorn Computers has implemented a printer server on their Econet – a local network. It is a network of BBC Microcomputers and the printer server runs on one of these micros (see Acorn, 1983). The printer server has been loaded on an EPROM which can be plugged into any one of the stations.

Having loaded the printer server, one must give that station a number which will be used by other stations in addressing the printer server. The client stations have been programmed to use 235 as the station number of the printer server. Therefore, if 235 is the number given to the printer server it will not be necessary to specify this number in commands from the client machines.

The printer server is designed to handle a small range of different printers, e.g. Olivetti JP101, Epson MX-80 and FX-80, Walters Microsystems WM2000, and some others. The appropriate printer code must be supplied at the server station on start-up of the system.

Since the printer server is an ordinary BBC Micro, one can use it for other tasks while the printer server is activated. However certain precautions must be taken (e.g. never press BREAK) in order to ensure smooth printing operations.

5.4 AN ELECTRONIC MAIL SERVER

In this section we will look at a distributed system which supports the exchange of mail. Grapevine was designed at Xerox Palo Alto Research Center as a distributed, replicated system supporting message delivery,

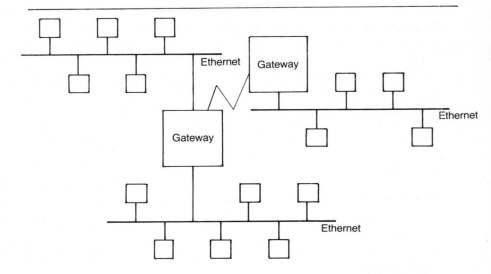

Fig. 5.8 An internetwork of Ethernets. Adapted from Birrell, A.D., Levin, R., Needham, R.M. and Schroeder, M.D., 1982, 'Grapevine: An exercise in Distributed Computing', *Commun ACM*, **25**, 4(April), 260–274, Copyright 1982, Association for Computing Machinery, Inc.

naming, authentication, resource location and access control services (Birrell et al, 1982; Schroeder et al, 1984). The system is implemented as an internetwork of LANs which link Ethernets from coast-to-coast in the USA to Canada and to England (see Figure 5.8). Its primary use is the delivery of electronic mail. It is implemented as two server systems: a message server and a registration server.

The message service supports the exchange of digital mail among the users of the host computers. The server allows the sender to package mail to named recipients and present it to its delivery mechanism. The delivery mechanism transfers the message from the sender to an internal buffer, called an *inbox*, for each recipient. When ready, the recipient can access the mail in his inbox. Grapevine does not interpret the messages that it delivers. The clients do the interpretation.

The registration service supports the resource location, authentication and access control functions. A register of named services, e.g., printer servers, file servers, is kept together with the control data to regulate the use of these services.

Grapevine is **replicated**, which means that it is implemented as a collection of cooperating servers all providing a more or less equal service. There is a registration database maintained by Grapevine to facilitate the reconciliation of names with the corresponding entities such as users, machines, services, distribution lists and access control lists. Distribution lists name groups of message recipients.

The registration service allows the following functions:

(a) *Authentication:* any client can determine the authenticity of an individual.
(b) *Membership:* a client can determine whether a name is included in some group. Membership of a group allows certain access control considerations.
(c) *Resource location:* this allows the determination of service addresses, and the location of inbox sites for message delivery and retrieval.
(d) *Registration database update and inquiry:* for updating and inspecting the registration database.

The delivery service allows the following functions:

(a) *Message acceptance:* the client uses this function to transfer a message from the sender to Grapevine's delivery service. When Grapevine acknowledges its acceptance of the message, the client can proceed to do something else.
(b) *Message polling:* an individual can have his inboxes inspected to determine whether there are messages to be retrieved. No password authentication is necessary here.
(c) *Message retrieval:* the client uses this function to obtain all messages from the inboxes of the named individual. Password authentication is necessary for this action.

The registration database is divided into registries which correspond to logical groupings in the user community. These groups may be determined by location, organization or application. These registries are replicated in several different registration servers, although no registration server contains all the registries. Individuals carry two-parameter names: a registry name and a unique name within registry.

The message servers contain inboxes of the recipients of mail. Each recipient has inboxes on at least two message servers, thus providing multiple delivery paths.

Sending mail generally involves the following steps (see Figure 5.9):

(a) The client packages the message from a user to a named recipient and passes it on to Grapevine delivery service.
(b) A registration server is contacted.
(c) Grapevine uses the registration service to locate a message server M (this message server need not contain the inboxes of the named recipient).
(d) The message server M receives the message.
(e) The message server M contacts a registration server to determine the recipient's best inbox site, say message server S.
(f) The message server M then forwards the message to S (if there are more recipients M will have to repeat steps (e) and (f)).

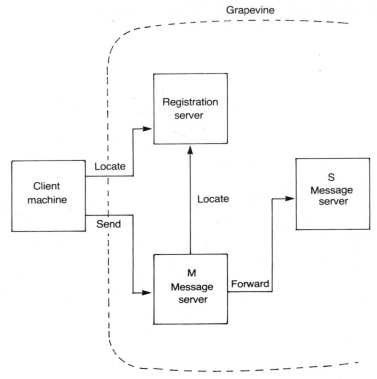

Fig. 5.9 Sending mail in Grapevine. Adapted from Birrell, A.D., Levin, R., Needham, R.M. and Schroeder, M.D., 1982, 'Grapevine: An exercise in Distributed Computing', *Commun ACM*, **25**, 4(April), 260–274, Copyright 1982, Association for Computing Machinery, Inc.

(g) Message server S stores the message in the recipient's inbox for later retrieval.

In order to retrieve mail, the following steps are taken (see Figure 5.10):

(a) Upon the user's request the client invokes the retrieval function of the Grapevine delivery service.
(b) A registration server is contacted to locate inbox sites for the recipient.
(c) The located message servers are then contacted to retrieve messages.
(d) The message server uses a registration server to authenticate the recipient before allowing retrieval of mail.

5.5 SUMMARY

Servers in the client-server network model permit users of a computer network to share a number of services irrespective of the location of these

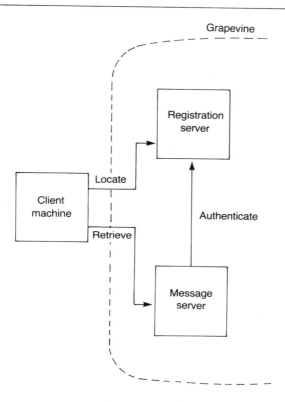

Fig. 5.10 Receiving mail in Grapevine. Adapted from Birrell, A.D., Levin, R., Needham, R.M. and Schroeder, M.D., 1982, 'Grapevine: An exercise in Distributed Computing', *Commun ACM*, **25**, 4(April), 260–274, Copyright 1982, Association for Computing Machinery, Inc.

services. In particular, if location transparency is one of the features of the server, the user need not be aware of the other stations that may be involved in satisfying his demands.

Some of the popular server systems are file servers, name servers, printer servers and mail servers. File servers allow the sharing of direct access storage devices; name servers map service names onto their addresses; printer servers offer the network stations the use of a common printer; and mail servers deliver electronic mail.

File servers have attracted the most attention in the research and development community and therefore some alternative design strategies have emerged. Some of the design issues include the distribution of function between the client and the server, the unit of access allowed to the client, the type of access and concurrency control, and the maintenance of recoverable files.

Communication protocols must be established in order to achieve a satisfactory level of client-server interaction. The underlying network protocols will have some effect on the higher level protocol model.

5.6 QUESTIONS

5.1 Indicate some advantages in having a file server rather than a local file-store.

5.2 What is location transparency?

5.3 What are the different units of access that file servers have been designed to support?

5.4 What are the effects of the choice of a particular unit of access on the design of the file server?

5.5 What facilities can a file server be extended to support if it allows a unit of access of:
(a) a page;
(b) a byte?

5.6 How does an identity based access control system differ from a capability-based system?

5.7 Discuss an approach for the allocation of storage to files in the file-store.

5.8 Distinguish between the three-message and the single shot protocols.

5.9 What is an idempotent request? Why must requests in the single shot protocol be idempotent?

5.10 What is an atomic transaction? Discuss the use of:
(a) the shadow-page technique;
(b) the undo/redo log in the implementation of atomic transactions.

5.11 What is the commit point of a transaction? How is an intentions log used in the completion of committed transactions?

5.12 Indicate any differences that you have observed in the design of the two file servers: XDFS and CFS.

5.13 What is an 'undeletable' file? Give one solution to the problem of the 'undeletable' file.

5.14 Discuss some advantages and disadvantages in having:
(a) a name server;
(b) a printer server.

5.15 Discuss the ways in which a name server and a mail server can cooperate.

5.16 Suggest other servers, not discussed in this chapter, that you think might be useful in a network environment.

5.17 Assume that a fixed disk with the characteristics outlined below was available to build a file server system supporting page access to files with local filing systems. Design the data tables to manage file mapping and storage allocation for 1000 users (mainly students) with an average of 10 files each. Comment on the format of the FID and a mechanism for access control.

Characteristics of the fixed disk:

Total capacity	513 Megabytes
2 moving heads per surface	
1.2 Megabytes per sec peak transfer rate	
No. of surfaces for data recording	20
No. of cylinders	835
No. of blocks per cylinder	120

5.7 REFERENCES

1 Acorn Computers Limited, 1983. *Econet Printer Server Manager's Guide.* Cambridge: Baddeley Associates.

2 Birrell, A.D., Levin, R., Needham, R.M. and Schroeder, M.D., 1982. 'Grapevine: An Exercise in Distributed Computing', *Communications of the ACM*, **25**, 4(April), 260–274.

3 Brown, M.R., Kolling, K.N. and Taft, E.A., 1985. 'The Alpine File System', *ACM Transactions on Computer Systems*, **3**, 4(Nov), 261–293.

4 Lampson, B.W., 1981. 'Atomic Transactions' in *Distributed Systems: Architecture and Implementation, an Advanced Course*, pp. 246–264 (ed. B.W. Lampson). Berlin: Springer Verlag.

5 Mitchell, J.G., 1982. *File Servers for local area networks.* Xerox PARC Palo Alto, California.

6 Needham, R.M. and Herbert, A.J., 1982. *The Cambridge Distributed Computing System*, London: Addison-Wesley.

7 Schroeder, M.D., Birrell, A.D. and Needham, R.M., 1984. 'Experience with Grapevine: The Growth of a Distributed System', *ACM Transactions on Computer Systems*, **2**, 1(Feb), 3–23.

8 Sturgis, H.E., Mitchell, J.G. and Israel, J., 1980. 'Issues in the design and use of a distributed File System', *ACM SIGOPS Operating Systems Review*, **14**, 3(Jul), 55–69.

9 Svobodova, L., 1984. 'File Servers for Network-Based Distributed Systems', *ACM Computing Surveys*, **16**, 4, 353–398.

10 Utting, I., 1984. 'Distributed High Quality Printer Servers'. University of Kent at Canterbury, Workshop on the Cambridge Ring.

CHAPTER SIX

DISTRIBUTED DATABASE SYSTEMS

Distributed database systems form an integral part of the work going on in distributed computing. In fact, it is one area that has generated a considerable amount of interest. We merely scratch the surface in this chapter. Although this discussion is for those who have already been introduced to database technology, some fundamentals have been included to facilitate the uninitiated. For a more comprehensive introduction refer to Date (1986). The reader with previous database knowledge can proceed directly to section 6.2.

6.1   SOME INTRODUCTORY CONCEPTS

An essential ingredient for the successful operation of an organization is accurate and timely information. Computer storage capabilities provide an efficient means for storing the individual data elements from which the information requirements can be met.

In many instances, the volume of data elements may be high, thus placing large demands on computer storage. The same data elements may serve different information applications within an organization. For example, in a manufacturing organization, data on inventory items may be needed for the purchasing, customer-ordering, accounts receivable and accounts payable applications. The earliest computerized business applications usually stored their own copies of the necessary data items thus generating a great deal of redundancy in data file contents.

Although this practice still exists, an increasingly popular approach is the storage of all the data items pertaining to the whole organization in one central pool called a ***database***. This not only serves to remove unnecessary redundancies but also reduces the need for repeated updates to preserve data integrity across the organization.

Some of the key questions that must be answered when designing an information system are

(a) who will be using it?
(b) what data structures will be employed?
(c) how are the data items related? and
(d) how will the data items be stored?

These factors have all been addressed in database technology and we will review them briefly in the following subsections.

6.1.1 Separate views

A database is built to support many different applications. Each application must have the facility to select from the database the data elements that are appropriate. Therefore a mechanism must exist to allow the separate applications different views of the data. Such a facility is incorporated in the ***external level*** of the database system.

Each user has an external view that is consistent with that user's needs. For example, the information stored in a database on a *part* may include *part #, part name, supplier of part, price, quantity in stock*. The user who is calculating the bill may be interested only in *part #* and *price*. While the one who is generating the purchase order may be interested only in *part #, supplier of part* and *quantity in stock*. These are the separate external views.

At the same time there has to be a global view of the database which embodies all the necessary interrelationships among the data elements. This global view must be so designed as to support the individual user views which exist at the external level. This overall view is afforded at the *conceptual level* of the database.

This is an abstract logical view that is separate from the data actually stored. With respect to the parts example above, the conceptual viewer sees all the data items that pertain to the entity part, as well as how each part is related to other entities that may be in the database.

Thirdly, there is the *internal level* of the database i.e. how the data are physically organized. The aim at this level is to implement an organization that would support the logical structure of the database. The organization must facilitate insertions and deletions, and provide satisfactory response times on transactions.

A strategy in database construction is to modularize the implementation to allow operations to proceed at each of the levels without being seriously affected by changes at another level. This characteristic of database design is called ***data independence***.

6.1.2   Database structure

Models that have been used to build database systems are: the *inverted list model*; the *hierarchical* or *tree model*; the *network* or *plex model*; and the *relational model*.

However, before any model of the data can be constructed, there has to be some definition of the component parts of that model. Database technology recognizes that there are certain objects which form the basic source of data for any organization. For example, in a manufacturing organization, these objects include suppliers, parts, customers, etc. These objects are usually referred to as *entities*. Each entity has certain *attributes* which permit distinction between entities of the same type. For example, the attributes of the supplier may be supplier number, name, address, etc. A particular combination of attribute values for a given entity is usually referred to as a *record* or an *entity occurrence*.

The logical structure of the database will therefore define the relationships among entities and facilitate the retrieval of particular attributes of any of the entities from the database.

The inverted list model

An inverted list system contains files of data records and a collection of attribute indexes facilitating sequential and random access to those data records. Indexed files have an index which associates the unique ID or *primary key* of the record with the address of that record. If, in addition to this primary index, there are indexes which associate other non-unique attributes or *secondary keys* of the record with the primary key or address of the record, then that system is regarded as inverted. Direct entry to the file is now allowed through an attribute other than the primary key.

For example, a simple inverted list database system containing information on oil wells can take the following form:

OIL WELL FILE

well no.	location	rating	operational cost	barrels per day	other details
100	site 1	6	10000	6000	
200	site 3	5	20000	10000	
300	site 2	7	12000	8900	
400	site 5	5	10000	7000	

PRIMARY INDEX

well no.	address
100	block 1
200	block 1
300	block 2
400	block 2

SECONDARY INDEXES

rating	*well no.*	*operational cost*	*well no.*
5	200, 400	10000	100, 400
6	100	12000	300
7	300	20000	200

barrels per day	*well no.*
6000	100
7000	400
8900	300
10000	200

Where the volume of data elements stored is large, as in some document searching systems, several strategies can be used to optimize handling of queries (Martin, 1977).

The hierarchical model
In the *hierarchical model*, relationships among entities are expressed as a tree structure. Figure 6.1 shows such a structure with the parent or root node being the supplier and the children being the parts. Tree structures

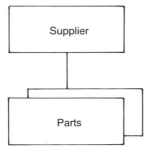

Fig. 6.1 Relationship between supplier and part expressed as a tree structure

permit only one parent for each child, which is a serious restriction when one considers that many records can be inherently related to more than one parent, e.g. one part can be supplied by more than one supplier.

Access to data elements is usually through the root record occurrence and, in fact, dependent records do not exist without a root. Simple tree structures are, therefore, not considered as the best model for database design. However, this approach was popular during the early development of database technology.

The network model
The network model removes the restriction of dependent elements having only one superior. As Figure 6.2 indicates, every record can have any

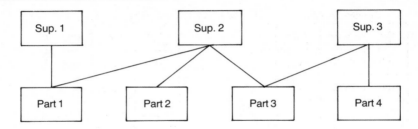

Fig. 6.2   A network structure in which the child has more than one parent

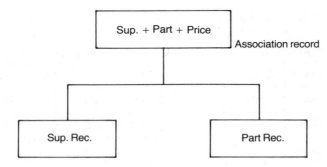

Fig. 6.3   The intersection data in the association record affords a tree arrangement in the network model

number of parents as well as any number of children. This structure can adequately represent many inherent relationships among data entities.

A particular parent record may be distinguishable from another parent of the same child by some unique association with that child. For example, the suppliers of the same part may have different unit prices on their part. It is necessary to form another record to indicate this association (see Figure 6.3). This association record then forms a root node linking the appropriate part and supplier records thus facilitating the information retrieval process.

The network model has a significant part in the historical development of database technology, and may still be employed in some environments. However, it is now superseded by the more elegant relational model which is less complex to organize.

The relational model
The elegance of the relational model is the result of its mathematical foundation. It arose primarily from the work of Codd (1970) who used the mathematical theory of relations to model data structures for large databases.

Supplier relation

S#	Name	City
100	JOHN	POS
200	DOE	NY

Unit price relation

S#	P#	Price
100	1011	$0.50
100	1300	$1.50
200	1123	$0.60
200	1246	$0.70

Parts relation

P#	Pname	Quantity
1011	Bolt	400
1123	Nut	400
1246	Screw	600
1300	Nail	500

Dictionary

Relat.	Locat.	#Tups	T-size
Sup	Site1	800	10
Part	Site2	15000	10
Price	Site3	10000	3

Fig. 6.4 The tabular structure in a relational model

In this model the data elements are stored as tables which are called *relations* (see Figure 6.4). The rows are called *tuples* and the columns are the *attributes*. Each attribute (data field) entry is chosen from a particular set of values called its *domain*. For example, if a part can have any of four colors, then these four colors make up the domain from which the attribute value, color, is selected.

A positive feature of the relational approach is that information about these relations can also be stored as a relation. The relation describing the relations is called a *dictionary* (see Figure 6.4). The use of this simple tabular form throughout the database allows uniform management and operation across the entire system.

6.1.3 Query processing

In this section, the relational model will be the only approach considered. In fact, wherever the discussion involves reference to database structure, the relational model will be the one presented. This model has attracted considerable attention, in both research and production environments, and has assumed dominance over the other models among the more recent database designers.

Query processing, retrieving information on demand from the database, involves accessing or manipulation of relations. *Query languages* are provided for the retrieval of information from the database. The elements of the language are determined usually by the choice of one of two underlying principles, namely **relational algebra** and **relational calculus**.

In a language based on a relational algebra, the procedure for answering a query is explicitly specified. Relational calculus languages require merely that the conditions to be satisfied by the answer are specified.

Relational algebra

Relational algebra contains operators which manipulate one or more relations in order to produce another relation. For example, if ∗ operates on two relations, A and B, then a third relation, C, is formed when the following expression is evaluated

$$C := A * B.$$

Some operators that have been defined are *select, project, product, union, intersect, difference, divide* and *join*. A brief definition of these operations follows.

Select has a single relation (table) as its operand. From this relation, specified tuples (rows) are extracted.

Project has one relation (table) as its operand. From this relation, specified attributes (columns) are extracted.

Product has two relations as its operands. A new relation is built by forming all the possible concatenated pairs of tuples where a pair includes a tuple from each of the two relations. For example if

$$A = \begin{vmatrix} a & x \\ b & y \end{vmatrix} \text{ and } B = \begin{vmatrix} d \\ e \end{vmatrix}$$

then:

$$A \text{ } product \text{ } B = \begin{vmatrix} a & x & d \\ a & x & e \\ b & y & d \\ b & y & e \end{vmatrix}$$

Union has two relations as its operands. A new relation is formed consisting of all tuples in either or both of the two operands. For example if

$$R1 = \begin{vmatrix} a & b \\ c & d \end{vmatrix} \text{ and } R2 = \begin{vmatrix} c & d \\ r & s \end{vmatrix}$$

then:

$$R1 \; union \; R2 = \begin{array}{cc} a & b \\ c & d \\ r & s \end{array}$$

Intersect has two relations as its operands. A new relation is formed consisting of all the tuples in both operands. For example, using R1 and R2 as defined

$$R1 \; intersect \; R2 = \begin{array}{cc} c & d \end{array}.$$

Difference has two relations as its operands. It forms a new relation consisting of all the tuples that are in the first relation and not in the second relation. For example if

$$A = \begin{array}{cc} a & b \\ c & d \\ e & f \end{array} \quad \text{and } B = \begin{array}{cc} e & f \end{array}$$

then

$$A \; difference \; B = \begin{array}{cc} a & b \\ c & d \end{array}$$

Divide has two relations as operands: one relation with two attributes (binary), and the other with a single attribute (unary). The result is a unary relation which is formed by extracting all the values of one attribute of the binary relation, which match in the other attribute with all values in the unary relation. For example if

$$A = \begin{array}{cc} a & y \\ b & x \\ c & z \\ b & y \end{array} \quad \text{and } B = \begin{array}{c} x \\ y \end{array}$$

then

$$A \; divide \; B = \begin{array}{c} b \end{array}.$$

Join has two relations as its operands plus some condition that specified attributes must satisfy. A new relation is built consisting of concatenated pairs of tuples. A pair includes a tuple from each relation and that tuple must have satisfied the specified condition.

The three operators not yet illustrated – *select, project, join* – are those most commonly used. We will look at them in the following example.

Consider the query: 'What are the names of suppliers in NY who supply screws at a unit price less than $1.00?'

As we have seen above, the relational algebra provides operators for

Rprice

S#	P#	Price
100	1011	$0.50
200	1123	$0.60
200	1246	$0.70

(a)

Rpart

S#	P#	Pname	Quantity	Price
100	1011	Bolt	400	$0.50
200	1123	Nut	400	$0.60
200	1246	Screw	600	$0.70

(b)

Rscrew

S#	P#	Pname	. . . .	Price
200	1246	Screw	. . . .	$0.70

(c)

Rsupplier

S#	Name	City	P#	Pname	. .	Price
200	Doe	NY	1246	Screw	. .	$0.70

(d)

Rname

Name	City
Doe	NY

(e)

Fig. 6.5 Restriction of "unit price" relation produces 'rprice' in (a); join of 'parts' and 'rprice' produces 'rpart' in (b); restriction of 'rpart' produces 'rscrew' in (c); join of 'supplier' and 'rscrew' produces 'rsupplier' in (d); projection of 'rsupplier' produces 'rname' in (e)

manipulating the relations from which the answer will be derived. The procedure for executing this query (Q1) can take the following form:

An operator is needed to extract the tuple from the relation *unit price* where attribute *price* 'is less than $1.00'.

The result is Figure 6.5a. This is the select operator which is sometimes called *restriction* or *selection*.

Another operator is needed to merge the tuples in the relation *parts* with the relation *rprice* such that entries from the common attribute Part no. are equal. This operation is the *join* and it produces Figure 6.5b. In fact, this join is usually referred to as an **equijoin** since the condition on the attribute values is equality.

This is followed by a selection from the relation *rpart* of the tuples whose attribute *pname* is 'screw' to produce the relation *rscrew* in Figure 6.5c.

A join of relation *supplier* and *rscrew* over the common attribute S $\#$ produces Figure 6.5d. From the relation *rsupplier*, it is now necessary to extract the supplier names from the tuple associating supplier name with city, where city is 'NY'. This is the project operator sometimes called *a projection* and the result is Figure 6.5e.

Hence it is observed that, in a language based on a relational algebra, operators are specified which manipulate relations to generate other relations or tables.

Relational calculus

Relational calculus is relatively close to **natural language**. There are two streams of formulation: **tuple calculus** and **domain calculus**.

In a tuple calculus, there is the concept of a **tuple variable**. The value of a tuple variable must be a tuple from a particular relation. The tuple variable is said to 'range over' a given relation and hence it is sometimes called a '**range variable**'. The individual attributes of the tuple variable can be specified as components of that tuple. For example, if S is the tuple variable ranging over the relation supplier, then name and city attributes may be specified as S.name and S.city respectively.

A possible form that a query procedure for Q1 can take in a relational tuple calculus is

> Range of S is supplier;
> Range of P is parts;
> Range of SP is unit-price
> Retrieve S.name where
> $S.S\# = SP.S\#$ and $SP.P\# = P.P\#$ and
> SP.price $< \$1.00$ and
> P.pname $=$ 'Screw' and S.city $=$ 'NY'

In domain calculus, there is the notion of the **domain variable**. The domain variable assumes values from a particular domain. The aim is to identify tuples in a specified relation for which certain attribute values are equal to given domain values. For example, the format:

$$R(A_1 : v_1, A_2 : v_2, \ldots)$$

expresses a condition which is to be applied to relation, R. That condition is true if, and only if, there exists a tuple in R having for all *i* the domain value v_i for the attribute A_i. v_i is the domain variable or it may be a constant.

The same query, Q1, may be expressed in the following form in a domain calculus:

> *Namex* is a domain variable for *name*
> *Sx* is a domain variable for *S#*
> *Px* is a domain variable for *P#*
> *Pricex* is a domain variable for *price*

Retrieve *Namex* where exists *Sx* exists *Px* exists *Pricex*
(suppliers (*S#* : *Sx*, *name* : *Namex*, city : 'NY')
and parts (*P#* : *Px*, *pname* : 'screw')
and unit price (*S#* : *Sx*, *P#* : *Px*, *price* : *Pricex*)
and price < "$1.00").

Notice that the conditions for the names required are specified. The way in which the query procedure is actually executed is not indicated in the relational calculus.

Irrespective of the type of language provided, the actual searching of the database is still of prime concern. The physical storage of the relations and the search and routing algorithms used can significantly affect the performance of the system.

6.1.4   Relation building

In this section some of the considerations which underly the design of a 'good' relation in a database will be introduced. This is often referred to as the 'database design' problem and is concerned with what items of data should be included in a relation and what should be located in other relations.

Two basic characteristics of a relation are:

(a) it contains no duplicate tuples; and
(b) all attribute values are atomic, i.e. single valued

It follows from (a) that each tuple in a relation is unique, and from (b) that an attribute value cannot be split into more than one data item. A relation satisfying (b) is said to be normalized. The process of converting an unnormalized relation to a normalized relation is called ***normalization***.

The normalized relation may still possess some undesirable properties which can be removed by applying further normalization steps. The normalized relation is regarded as being in *first normal form* (1NF); and (do not be startled) progressively more desirable forms that have been defined are *second normal form* (2NF), *third normal form* (3NF), *Boyce/Codd normal form* (BCNF), *fourth normal form* (4NF), and *fifth normal form* (5NF) (see Kent, 1983; Date, 1986). The overall aim is to achieve a database design which possesses no unnecessary (or harmful) redundancies and would, therefore, be less of a problem to update.

Several normalization algorithms have been described in the literature to facilitate the design exercise. A system has been proposed by Ceri and Gottlob (1986) that collects and integrates certain normalization algorithms. The system is implemented in the Prolog language and is claimed to be well suited both for the design of small databases and as a teaching aid.

6.1.5 Database storage

Direct access storage devices (DASDs) are the only suitable media for data storage in database systems. Although floppy disks can be used in small scale applications, large data volume and high activity systems require fast access, large capacity DASDs.

The distribution of data elements over the physical media is an important factor in the determination of performance levels. Frequently accessed data elements should require minimum search times. This may involve the storage of multiple copies to permit a choice of accessing the item nearest to the present read-head position. Wherever possible, the storage should be organized in a way that permits concurrent execution of queries. For example, different physical volumes may be used to permit parallel access of database contents.

A significant design task is the physical representation of the logical relations. The physical representation supports the logical structure, but at the same time it should be so independent of that logical structure to permit changes on one hand – logical or physical – without serious disruption on the other.

Methods of organization used include indexed sequential and indexed nonsequential files, chains, linked lists of several varieties (forward, backward, circular, multilist), and random storage techniques like hashing. The reader is referred to Martin (1977) for an extensive coverage of storage techniques.

6.2 THE CASE FOR DISTRIBUTION

Computer networks have created the opportunity to share large databases among many users who may be widely dispersed geographically. A local area network can interconnect the functionally distinct departments of large organizations. Adequate storage capabilities can be allocated to a single site for the purpose of operating a centralized database accessible by all the users of a network.

However, such a centralized arrangement makes the database vulnerable to failures at the site at which it resides. Variable communication delays, biases in the channel allocation method and routing algorithms can render an inequitable service to users of the network. In addition, depending on the demand for service, the centralized resource can suffer periods of saturation which can seriously degrade performance levels.

One solution is the distribution of the database. In this arrangement, the database is divided into a number of cooperating databases, each located at a separate site, and users of the database at any site are allowed to access both locally and remotely stored data. Such a system is called a *distributed database system* (DDBS).

An organization may contain many branches, as in the banking business. Each branch can store the data elements pertaining to their local customers on site. Therefore, the majority of the transactions should be handled by accessing the local database. However, customers must be allowed the privilege to use the facilities at other branches as well. In such circumstances, it would be useful to permit the remote branch to access the customers' accounts immediately even though it is stored in an off site database. Hence, we will have a system where the collection of local branch databases forms a DDBS accessible by all the branches. This is one example of the way in which a database system can be distributed. This matter is dealt with in more detail in section 6.3.

A DDBS has a number of advantages over a centralized database system. There is increased reliability with the spreading of the database over several sites. The database could be partitioned in such a way to locate sections closer to their areas of highest demand. This can improve transaction processing times. Furthermore, the distributed system can generate distribution of the communication traffic on the network and thus reduce the incidence of saturation at some central site.

Maintenance and upgrading of the database will benefit from the modular implementation of the distributed system. With some degree of replication (copies of modules held at separate locations) it is possible to redirect transactions when some site is temporarily off line. New modules can be added as the need arises.

The increasing availability of database management software for microcomputers, as well as the advances in hard disk technology for these computers, can be viewed as an added incentive for distributed database design (Egyhazy, 1984).

6.3   THE DISTRIBUTION PROBLEM AND PATTERN

The task of distribution involves deciding where to locate the relations in the database in order to provide the best level of service at minimum cost. In a network environment where transactions at individual sites are functionally distinct (transactions in the personnel department compared with those in the accounts department) or where transactions access mainly local data (local branches in the banking organization), the partitioning of the database may mirror this distinction. However, where the functions are not naturally distinct the partitioning is not as clear cut.

Irrespective of the form chosen for distribution, there has to be some underlying system which supports the storage of these logically related files across the network. This was discussed in the introduction to file server systems in Chapter 5 where it was observed that mechanisms had been incorporated in some servers to facilitate this distribution. In particular we saw, as an example, that XDFS allows the existence of multiple servers. These multiple servers are managed by a sort of supervisory server called the *coordinator*.

There are certain parameters that must be considered when undertaking the distribution of a database. These parameters are:

(a) the number of participating hosts or sites,
(b) the storage facilities at the different sites,
(c) the channel capacity along the communication links, and
(d) the cost factor relating to all aspects of the design.

In addition, the volume and activity characteristics of the database must be taken into account.

Volume and activity

Volume pertains to the number of relations, the number of tuples in a relation, and the number of attributes within the tuples. Large numbers of data items will necessitate huge storage capacities.

Activity pertains to the distribution of transactions across the network: what type of transaction occurs where, how frequently and what are the response time constraints on the transactions. By 'type of transactions' is meant, What is the nature of the processing and what database elements are needed to complete the transaction?

The number of participating hosts

The number of hosts accessing the distributed database will affect the pattern of distribution. One of the major objectives in the distribution is to provide a high level of availability. Users at a particular site should be unable to perceive delays when processing transactions which require remote access. One solution is to store a copy of the entire database at each site. However, the transaction activity generated by some sites may be so low that this full distribution cannot be justified.

Storage facilities

Storing copies of large portions of the database may increase availability. But this incurs a secondary storage cost which the system may not afford. Hence, in order to save on this cost, existing storage facilities may be used which may mean less duplication.

Communication load

In order to minimize the communication load the system should aim to maximize the local processing. This maximization of local processing is subject to the availability, at the local site, of the database fragments that are required.

A pattern

The distribution can assume any of the following forms: *replication, full partitioning, vertical partitioning* and *horizontal partitioning.*

Replication: In a replicated database each relation is stored at more than one location. If each location has a copy of all the relations, the database is *fully replicated.* On the other hand, if each relation is stored at only one location the database is *fully partitioned.*

Vertical partitioning: The relations are distributed vertically or in columns. In this system, subsets of attributes of a relation are stored at separate hosts. Each host will therefore contain some attributes for all the tuples of the relation.

Horizontal partitioning: The relations are distributed horizontally or in rows. In such a system, subsets of tuples of the relation are stored at separate hosts. Each host will, therefore, contain all the attributes for some of the tuples of a relation.

In the pursuit of greater system efficiency, it may be necessary to subdivide into even smaller fragments of the database. Development of algorithms for optimal database partitioning is currently under research. In fact, this is related to what is usually referred to as the 'file assignment problem': how to distribute files among storage nodes optimally in a computer network. Studies have shown that this is not an easy problem, but some models have been developed; and savings in time or cost could be significant if some near optimal assignment is made. The reader is referred to Dowdy and Foster (1982) for some details.

6.4   QUERIES AND UPDATES IN DDBS

Transactions in a distributed environment are of two types: *queries* which involve requests for information and *updates* which generate changes to data entries in the database. The partitioning of the database is aimed at optimizing the transaction processing. The system should provide the best level of service at minimum cost. However, this distribution introduces some complexities in the handling of updates. All copies of segments of the database must reflect the correct state of the database.

6.4.1   Queries

In a distributed environment, queries can either be processed locally or it may be necessary to access remote sites. The need to access remote sites introduces communication costs and can increase response time. Therefore, the major concern will be how to optimize query processing either to generate the least possible traffic on the communication channel, or to minimize the response time. Yu and Chang (1984) have presented some of the ideas that are pertinent to this optimization and the following discussion leans a little on their report.

The first phase of query processing can be called the *copy identification phase*. At this phase, the relations involved in the query must be identified. If there is only one copy stored of each relation, one merely has to locate them. If there are multiple copies, it is necessary to make an optimum selection. Although there are multiple copies they may not all be available. This will condition the selection. So too should the communication distance separating copies of all relations involved in the query. Information on the location of relations could be acquired through some 'dictionary' relation, which may be replicated at some known (possibly all) locations in order to increase reliability and decrease access times.

All the relations required for processing the query can be transmitted to a single host where all the processing can be done. The large volumes that may be involved in such a transfer make this an unattractive approach. Alternatively, all the processing that can be done at a single host can be done there and transmission of relations only takes place when a relation stored elsewhere is needed to complete an operation.

One strategy is to decompose the query into single relation subqueries and two relation subqueries. The single relation subqueries are then distributed to the appropriate sites. If the partitioning is horizontal or vertical, there is need for an even finer distribution. Furthermore, appropriate sites must be chosen to perform the 'join' operations for the two relation subqueries.

Site subresponses to these subqueries have to be coalesced at some predetermined location. Finally, the complete response has to be composed for the destination site. The choice of sites for all these operations may be influenced, primarily, by the size of relations involved in the transmissions.

As an example, let us refer to the query Q1 in section 6.1.3. Assume that the relations supplier, parts and unit price are at the separate sites, site 1, site 2 and site 3 respectively (see Figure 6.6). Assume further that the query originates at site 1. Single relation subqueries can be done at the resident sites, e.g.:

SQ1. 'Find $S\#$, supplier name where supplier city is "NY"; at site 1.'

The result of a selection is the relation:

$$SR1 = (200, \text{DOE}, \text{NY}, \dots).$$
SQ2. Find $P\#$ where *pname* = 'screw'; at site 2.

The result of a selection is the relation:

$$SR2 = (1246, \text{SCREW}, 600, \dots).$$
SQ3. Find $S\#$, $P\#$ where price $<$ \$1.00; at site 3.

IDPC—K

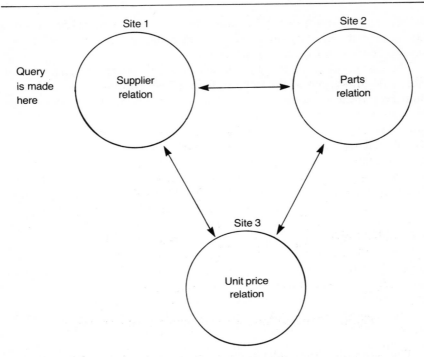

Query
is made
here

Site 1

Supplier
relation

Site 2

Parts
relation

Site 3

Unit price
relation

Fig. 6.6 Three relations of the DDBS at separate sites

The result of a selection is the relation

$$SR3 = (100, 1011, \$0.50)$$
$$(200, 1123, \$0.60)$$
$$(200, 1246, \$0.70).$$

That is the easy part. Now on to the two relation subqueries. SQ4. 'Find $S\#$ for suppliers who supply screws with a price $< \$1.00$'. Here we need inputs from site 2 (SR2) and site 3 (SR3). There is a choice between doing the join at site 2 or site 3 or even at site 1 (see Figure 6.7). A recommended strategy is to move the smaller relation. The join produces relation:

$$SR4 = (200, 1246, \$0.70, SCREW, 600, \ldots).$$

SQ5. 'Find supplier name where supplier is in "NY" and $S\#$ equals those obtained from the response to subquery, SQ4'. Since the response is needed at site 1 the response from SQ4 could be transferred to site 1 (see Figure 6.7) where the join and projection to determine supplier name could be performed.

From this example it is obvious that the join operation is the most critical. This has led to the definition of a new operation: the *semijoin*.

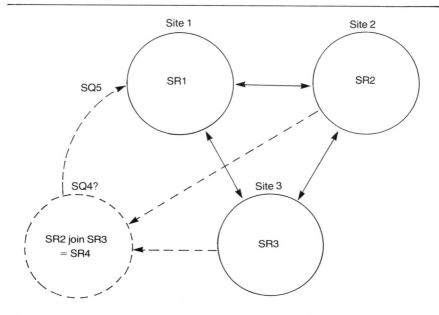

Fig. 6.7 The question is where to perform the join operations

The semijoin from relation R to relation S on the attribute A is equivalent to the join of R and S followed by a projection back onto the attributes of S. In other words, the resulting relation is the same as that obtained after a selection from S of those tuples which have values for attribute A that match values of attribute A in relation R.

For example, if we look again at Figure 6.5, we will see where the relation *rsupplier* in (d) was the result of a join of *supplier* and *rscrew* over attribute $S\#$. Alternatively, the semijoin from *rscrew* to *supplier* on the attribute $S\#$ produces the tuple

$$(200, DOE, NY, \ldots).$$

This is much shorter than the number of bytes required for *rsupplier* in Figure 6.5. Hence there can be savings in the storage and transmission of the result.

Instead of a join at SQ4 above, there could be a semijoin from the intermediate relation *SR2* at site 2 to the intermediate relation *SR3* at site 3 over the attribute $P\#$. This yields the intermediate relation

$$SRS = (200, 1246, \$0.70).$$

Since *SRS* is smaller than *SR4*, there can be savings in processing the subquery SQ5.

The way in which the semijoin is processed can also result in savings on the communications load. For example, in the processing of *SQ4*,

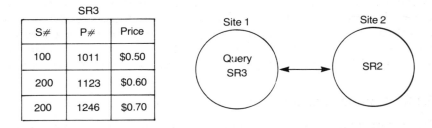

Fig. 6.8 A query is made at site 1 to join SR2 and SR3

assume that the relation, *SR2*, was sent to site 3. Instead, in a semijoin it is necessary to send only the values of attribute *P#*, which in this case is the single item '1246'.

However, the semijoin does not always prove better than the join. Let us assume that *SR3* is at site 1, *SR2* is at site 2 and a query is made at site 1 to join *SR2* and *SR3* on the attribute *P#* (see Figure 6.8). This could be done by requesting that site 2 send the relation *SR2* to site 1 where the join is performed.

A procedure using semijoin could take the following form. Site 1 sends a list of distinct attribute values of *P#* to site 2, i.e. 1011, 1123, 1246. At site 2, all tuples for which there is a match with these values on attribute *P#* are selected, i.e. the semijoin from *SR3* to *SR2* over attribute *P#* is performed. This yields the intermediate relation

$$SR32 = (1246, \text{SCREW}, 600, \ldots).$$

Finally *SR32* is transmitted to site 1 where the join is completed.

In comparing the join with the semijoin, it is clear that the semijoin is considerably more costly. In fact the intermediate relation *SR32*, which was obtained in the semijoin, is equal to *SR2* which was the only data transmitted in the join operation.

It is therefore desirable to be able to make an estimate of the sizes of intermediate relations before embarking on a particular procedure. Yu and Chang (1984) have described some estimation algorithms that may be used.

Even if the amount of data transmitted in processing the semijoin is less than that for the join, the number of messages exchanged in the semijoin operation may negate any gains in performance. The communication protocols in the network may cause the number of messages to have greater weight than the amount of data when determining the communication cost.

Another factor that must be considered is the distribution of processing power over the network. The fact that an intermediate relation can be obtained at a local site may reduce the communication load, but at the same time it increases the CPU load at that site. How well can this site deal with an increase in its processing load? Does this operation have high priority or would it have to join a long queue? Since indeterminacy in the response times cannot be accommodated in the DDBS, it may be necessary, at times, to ship the relation to another site for the processing.

6.4.2 Updates and integrity

Two major conditions in a distributed environment make the processing of updates a difficult task. One is the fact that concurrent transactions are allowed. If two updates are being processed for the same data item fields at the same time, what is the final state of the area updated? The other condition is the possible existence of multiple copies of sections of the database. The contents of the replicated partitions must be consistent.

Usually updates are made within the context of transactions that first read from the database, do some computation and then write new values to the database. Let Ri represent a read by transaction i and Wi represent a write by transaction i. Then concurrent processing of the two transactions 1 and 2 each with read and write operations can take, among others, the following sequences:

(a) $R1W1R2W2$
(b) $R1R2W1W2$
(c) $R1R2W2W1$.

(a) is safe, but (b) and (c) are not. For example, let transaction 1 represent a deposit of $100 to A's account while 2 represents a withdrawal of $100. With an initial sum of $300 in A's account, sequence (a) would leave the account showing $300, sequence (b) would leave the account showing $200, while sequence (c) would leave $400. Only sequence (a) did a correct update.

The update $W1$ in sequence (b) and the update $W2$ in sequence (c) are lost. This is an example of what is referred to as the *lost update* problem in concurrent transactions. Sequence (a) possesses a *serial* quality which has been shown always to generate correct results, i.e. each Ri must be immediately followed by its Wi.

Other problems associated with concurrent updates are the *uncommitted dependency* problem and the *inconsistent analysis* problem.

The uncommitted dependency problem arises when a transaction is allowed to access a data area that has been changed by another transaction

	Transaction picture				Database state	
	Transaction S			Transaction T	A	B
After step	A	B	sum	A		
1	$100				$100	$90
2			$100		$100	$90
3				$100	$100	$90
4				$120	$100	$90
5					$120	$90
6		$90			$120	$90
7			$190		$120	$90

Fig. 6.9 Inconsistent analysis. The committed transaction T generated an inconsistent state for the transaction S

but the change has not yet been committed. Since the update has not yet been committed, the possibility exists that it never will. Therefore, the first transaction could in fact have operated on data that 'never' existed.

The inconsistent analysis problem arises when a transaction performs some analysis based on an inconsistent state of the database. For example, let transaction S compute the present sum of two loan accounts, A and B, and let transaction T add $20 to A. A has value $100 and B has value $90. Assume the following sequence of operations (see Figure 6.9):

> S reads A
> S assigns to sum the value of A, i.e. $100
> T reads A
> T adds $20 to A (i.e. A is now $120)
> T commits
> S reads B
> S adds B to sum (i.e. sum is $190)

The committed transaction, T, generated an inconsistent state for the transaction, S. The result obtained by S is inconsistent with the database.

When the serial condition is not satisfied, these problems can arise. This safe property of serial processing has been extended and expressed in a formal theory of concurrency called **serializability theory** which formulates a precise condition for the correctness of concurrent transactions (Bernstein and Goodman, 1981).

6.4.2.1 Updates in a DDBS with no replication

First of all, in order to simplify things, consider the situation where there are no multiple copies of sections of the DDBS. However, simultaneous access by different users is allowed to the database. Therefore some concurrency control measure has to be adopted.

An objective of such a control measure should be:

(a) to permit parallel processing whenever there is no threat to the correctness of the database; and
(b) to enforce serial processing whenever the likelihood of corruption exists.

A strategy used is the *locking* mechanism. In the *no multiple copy* environment, the locking can be done at the site where the relation or database fragment resides. The locking ensures exclusive access to that area, which could be either the whole relation or some part thereof.

However, a transaction may need access to more than one relation. These relations may either all be at the same location or they may be distributed over different sites in the network. This can result in a deadlock if two transactions have each locked a relation needed by the other to complete. Adequate control measures must be introduced to avoid these deadlocks or indefinite delays.

An approach to the problem is to have a transaction lock all the needed relations before being allowed to proceed with the transaction. But how can this be achieved in the face of other transactions trying simultaneously to lock some or all of these very relations which are dispersed around the network? Some solutions have been adopted.

The centralized lock controller

A *centralized lock controller* is a central node which is allocated the function of granting lock requests. All transactions must first indicate the need to lock the required relations in the database to the central lock controller. If none of these relations is already locked, the lock request is granted; otherwise the new arrival must wait. The system is vulnerable to faults at the central site. Copies of the lock information could be spread over the net to increase reliability.

Timestamping

The fundamental principle here is to serialize transactions by tagging each transaction with a transaction number. The number could be formed by concatenating a host number with the time of day or *timestamp*. If the host initiates only one transaction during the clock 'tick' (the smallest time interval that is recorded – an interval of, say, 1 microsecond) the transaction numbers can be unique across the network.

A transaction is not processed until all the hosts involved have agreed on a particular one, and have locked out any other transaction attempting to use the same relations (or whatever the level of locking is). This agreement can be achieved through a series of 'lock request' broadcasts to all participating hosts.

The number of hosts, n say, involved in the transaction is determined by the initiating host who locks the local relation and broadcasts the transaction number, the number of participating hosts, and a 'please lock' request to the other $n - 1$ hosts. If a host does not already have that relation locked, it locks it and rebroadcasts the transaction number and the 'please lock' requests. Therefore, when all the hosts have received $n - 1$ lock requests for that transaction number, processing can begin.

If, during this process, a 'please lock' request is received for a lower transaction number, the previous one is queued and the new arrival is accepted for processing. Higher numbered arrivals are ignored. You should try to demonstrate, as an exercise, that all participating hosts will eventually agree on the same transaction.

6.4.2.2 Updates in a replicated DDBS

Let us now consider the replicated database, i.e. relations or fragments are duplicated at separate sites. A timestamping algorithm can also work here. All copies of the relations or fragments involved in the update transaction can be included in the lock agreement. This means that, in spite of there being multiple copies, no access is allowed to any, until updates to all copies are complete.

Majority consensus

This use of timestamps can be incorporated into another scheme called *majority consensus* (Thomas, 1979). When an update is applied, its timestamp is recorded. Timestamped transactions are broadcast to all hosts holding copies of the relation. If timestamps do not match with previous entries, the updates are accepted to be applied only if there is acceptance by the majority. In this way, the transaction held by a minority of the hosts is forced to *back-off*, thus giving way to the majority holder.

Primary node

A further approach is the notion of a *primary node* or *primary site*. In this scheme, a single node is identified as the first site where the update is performed (Ullman, 1982).

This concept builds on the geographically clustered behaviour of updates. For example, in a network of bank branches, each branch will deal with many more transactions pertaining to its local accounts than with transactions for a remote branch. Hence, each branch can be allocated as the primary site for all updates done to their accounts.

The update is then broadcast to the other nodes which perform the update and then send acknowledgments back to the primary node. There are variations on how processing of transactions is controlled during this update phase.

Concurrency control algorithms are continually being proposed and discussed in the research literature. The interested reader is directed, in the main, to the 'ACM Transactions on Database Systems' and the 'IEEE Transactions on Software Engineering'.

6.5 PARTITION FAILURES

The problems that relate to the temporary unavailability of any of the database sites or partitions will be considered in this section. This unavailability can arise from failures in the communication link with that site or a crash due to hardware or software malfunction at the site itself (Davidson, 1984).

A fully partitioned DDBS would be very vulnerable to such failure, since for the duration of the partition down-time, there will be no access allowed to a part of the database. To increase the robustness of the system it may be necessary to have some degree of replication and, in some environments, it is desirable to have full replication.

Of major concern in the event of these failures are:

(a) what is the state of transactions that would normally use that partition? and
(b) how is it possible to restore the failed partition, when it comes on stream again, to a state consistent with the rest of the database?

The concept of atomicity in transaction processing, as discussed in section 5.1.4, is useful in the face of failures to subsets of the database. A transaction either completes successfully (*commits*), or has no effect. The system must be able to *back-out* (or *roll back*) transactions that cannot be committed and complete those transactions, with minimum delay, that cannot be aborted.

The notion of backing out a transaction involves undoing any modification that may have been done by the incomplete transaction and allowing future restart of that transaction. Backing out at a particular site is facilitated by supporting recoverable objects. These are implemented by using techniques involving shadow pages, undo/redo logs, intentions logs and other related control records (Haerder and Reuter, 1983).

In a replicated DDBS, it may be necessary to update all copies of the database fragment at the same time. If the transaction fails, all the sites involved must undo or roll back. If the transaction is successful then all the sites must commit and complete the transaction. The *two phase commit* (Gray, 1978) permits all the copies of the database fragments always to reflect the outcome of the transaction.

The two phase commit scheme requires a coordinator to maintain a record of the state of the transaction. In the first phase the coordinator sends a 'go either way' or 'prepare' message to all the participating sites. On receipt of this message, each site fulfills its local requirements for the support of atomicity in the transaction.

When each site has succeeded in doing this it responds with a 'ready' or 'OK' message to the coordinator, otherwise its response will be 'abort' or 'not OK'. If all the responses received by the coordinator are positive, the coordinator will atomically change the state of the transaction to commit and begin the second phase by issuing a 'commit' message to the cooperating sites.

If there was a 'not OK' response in the first phase, or there was no response before some time-out, the coordinator will inform the sites to roll back. The coordinator waits until it has received responses to its second phase messages from all the sites before the transaction is considered complete. Any failure during the whole exercise generates a restart procedure based on the state of the transaction as maintained in the coordinator's log.

This immediate update system demands that transactions must see all copies before updating. This can seriously restrict the availability of the DDBS, and seems to run counter to one of the goals of distribution. Hence, an alternative strategy is to allow immediate updates to single copies and subsequent updates to the others.

Among the additional features that can be provided is that of continuing a transaction at another site if the partition that is presently being used fails. Indeed, in some systems, it may be highly desirable or even absolutely necessary to continue or restart the transaction at an alternative site. For example, one would not like to abort a military command system in the face of an enemy attack.

In such a replicated system, a site failure would mean that updates made to copies of relations held elsewhere will not be recorded at the failed site. When the site comes back 'on the air', a recovery process must be undertaken to ensure that it is made equal with the rest of the database.

The fundamental steps here are to identify the changes that were made during the failure, and to initiate a series of update transactions from the correct sites to the repaired site. During these updates, the relevant relations or fragments should be locked to avoid unpredictable modifications to the data fields. The identification of the updates is facilitated by proper timekeeping logs, indicating when changes were made and when the crash occurred, held at the participating hosts.

There are other issues pertinent to recovery that are handled in the communication protocols. For example, how do the other hosts know that a failure has occurred? We cannot expect a dead site to report that it has died. A lack of response within a certain time interval is a good indication that something has gone wrong. What happens if a suspected failure was not a failure at all, but rather an unusual delay in the arrival of some response? Here we have to rely on some unique message identification system in order to associate responses with requests accurately and to spot the duplicate requests which turn up later.

6.6 SOME EXAMPLE SYSTEMS

6.6.1 SDD-1

SDD-1, a System for Distributed Databases, was developed at the Computer Corporation of America, and it is claimed to be the first general purpose distributed database system ever developed (Rothnie Jr et al, 1980; Bernstein et al, 1981; Ceri and Pelagatti, 1984). It was initiated in 1976 and the first version was released in 1978. It runs on a collection of PDP-10s that are linked via ARPANET.

SDD-1 is a replicated database that supports location transparency. Its query optimizer uses the semijoin operator extensively to reduce the communication cost. It updates all copies of database fragments immediately and uses timestamping for concurrency control.

SDD-1 maintains a fully replicated '***directory locator***' at the top level in its address mapping system. Recovery is supported by a variant of the two phase commit protocol.

6.6.2 R*

R* (pronounced 'R star') was developed at IBM's San José Research Laboratory as a distributed version of their relational database, System R. In fact, R* consists of multiple cooperating copies of System R running on a set of IBM mainframes.

There is no replication in the current version, therefore update propagation does not arise. It provides location transparency and controls concurrency by locking the single copy of the object being accessed. Recovery is supported by a two phase commit technique.

R* does not use semijoins; it considers both the local processing cost and the data communication cost in its query optimization. It enumerates many strategies for performing joins and chooses the one with the least cost (Ceri and Pelagatti, 1984; Yu and Chang, 1984; Date, 1983).

6.6.3 Distributed INGRES

Distributed INGRES was developed at the University of California, Berkeley as a distributed version of their relational database, University INGRES (Stonebraker, 1979; Date, 1983). It runs on a network of PDP-11s, and supports location transparency, horizontal partitioning and replication.

It provides two approaches to update propagation. One offers primary node updating, and the other immediate update of all copies. A locking system is used to control concurrency, and recovery is supported by a two phase commit protocol.

Distributed INGRES considers both data communication cost and local processing cost in its query optimization. Queries are decomposed into a sequence of subqueries with the objective of minimizing the overall cost. It aims to maximize parallelism and to exploit the redundancy in data storage.

6.7 SUMMARY

Computer networks have created opportunities for the sharing of information, both at the local organizational level and the wider environment of public data enquiry systems. Distributed database system technology has been developed to exploit these opportunities.

Although there exists a choice of basic data structures from the inverted list, hierarchical, network and relational models, there has been a noticeable preference for the relational approach. This trend is due mainly to the elegance and simplicity of the relational model, based, as it is, on proven mathematical principles.

Several design issues must be dealt with in the implementation of a distributed database system. There is the problem of how to divide the database among the hosts. Should each host have a complete copy of the database, or on the other hand, should there be no multiple copies, instead each host has the only copy of some fragment of the database? When there are multiple copies, special techniques must be employed to handle updates. If all updates are to be done at the same time, all participating sites must first reach agreement on which update is to be done. A primary node technique can be used when it is not required to do all the updates immediately.

The handling of transactions in a network environment demands special control measures to ensure database integrity. Simultaneous access by separate transactions to the same data items can leave the database in an indeterminate state. Concurrency control algorithms must be employed to regulate the transaction and so avoid database corruption. Two common techniques are locking and timestamping.

The distributed database is susceptible to failures in the communication links as well as software and hardware malfunction at the individual sites. Crash recovery mechanisms must be adopted to ensure database consistency in the face of such breakdowns. The two phase commit protocol, or some variant thereof, has been used to facilitate recovery.

In spite of all of these difficulties, distributed databases are still viable systems and many researchers are engaged in serious study both to improve and develop techniques for distributed database design and implementation. Some notable operational systems are SDD-1, R*, and Distributed INGRES.

6.8　QUESTIONS

6.1　Distinguish among the following three levels of a database system: external, conceptual and internal.

6.2　Describe briefly the following database models: inverted list, hierarchical, network, and relational.

6.3　What is a query language? Distinguish between a query language based on relational algebra, and a query language based on relational calculus.

6.4　Use Figure 6.5 in performing the following operations:
(a) join the supplier relation and unit price relation over attribute $S\#$;
(b) perform a selection on the parts relation where the attribute quantity is less than '600';
(c) project all the relations and their location from the dictionary relation.

6.5　What does the term 'normalization of a relation' mean?

6.6　What is a distributed database system? Indicate some advantages that a distributed database system has over a centralized system.

6.7　Define the terms replication, vertical partitioning, and horizontal partitioning as used in a relational distributed database system.

6.8　Construct an employee relation for a large construction firm. Assume that existing departments are civil engineering, electrical engineering, mechanical engineering and accounting. Each department has a micro-computer with considerable fixed disk storage connected to a LAN. Give a rationale for distributing the employee relation
(a) horizontally,
(b) vertically.

6.9　Discuss the use of the semijoin operation in query optimization.

6.10　Discuss a strategy for query optimization that does not involve the semijoin operation.

6.11　Briefly explain the following problems which arise in concurrent transactions:
(a) lost update;
(b) uncommitted dependency; and
(c) inconsistent analysis.

6.12　Discuss the use of the following techniques in concurrency control for a distributed database system:
(a) a centralized lock controller;
(b) timestamping.

6.13 Explain the implementation of an update propagation system that uses:
(a) majority consensus;
(b) primary node.

6.14 Demonstrate the use of a two phase commit protocol as a mechanism for distributed database recovery.

6.15 From the brief reports on SDD-1, R* and Distributed INGRES what similarities and differences are observed?

6.9 REFERENCES

1 Bernstein, P.A. and Goodman, N., 1981. 'Concurrency control in distributed database systems', *ACM Computing Surveys*, **3**, 2(June), 185–221.

2 Bernstein, P.A., et al, 1981. 'Query Processing in a System for Distributed Databases (SDD-1)', *ACM Transactions on Database Systems*, **6**, 4(Dec), 602–625.

3 Ceri, S. and Goťtlob, G., 1986. 'Normalization of Relations and Prolog', *Communications of the ACM*, **29**, 6(June), 524–544.

4 Ceri, S. and Pelagatti, G., 1984. *Distributed Databases, Principles and Systems*. New York: McGraw Hill.

5 Codd, E.F., 1970. 'A relational model of data for large shared data banks', *Communications of the ACM*, **13**, 6(June), 377–387.

6 Date, C.J., 1983. *An Introduction to Database Systems, Vol. 2*. Reading, Massachusetts: Addison-Wesley Pub. Co.

7 Date, C.J., 1986. *An Introduction to Database Systems, Vol. 1* (fourth edition). Reading, Massachusetts: Addison-Wesley Pub. Co.

8 Davidson, S.B., 1984. 'Optimism and consistency in partitioned distributed database systems', *ACM Transactions on Database Systems*, **9**, 3(Sept), 456–481.

9 Dowdy, L.W. and Foster, D.V., 1982. 'Comparative models of the file assignment problem', *ACM Computing Surveys*, **14**, 2(June), 287–313.

10 Egyhazy, C.J., 1984. 'Microcomputers and relational database management systems: A new strategy for decentralizing databases', *DATABASE*, **16**, 1, 15–20.

11 Gray, J.N., 1978. 'Notes on database operating systems', *Lecture Notes in Computer Science, 60*, pp. 393–481. Berlin: Springer-Verlag. (Also Technical Report RJ2188, IBM San José Research Lab., San Jose, Calif., Feb.)

12 Haerder, T. and Reuter, A., 1983. 'Principles of transaction-oriented database recovery', *ACM Computing Surveys*, **15**, 4(Dec), 287–317.

13 Kent, W., 1983. 'A simple guide to five normal forms in Relational Database theory', *Communications of the ACM*, **26**, 2.

14 Martin, J., 1977. *Computer Database Organization* (second edition). Englewood Cliffs: Prentice Hall Inc.

15 Rothnie Jr, J.B. et al, 1980. 'Introduction to a System for Distributed Databases' (SDD-1), *ACM Transactions on Database Systems*, **5**, 1(Mar), 1–17.

16 Stonebraker, M.R., 1979. 'Concurrency Control and Consistency of Multiple Copies in Distributed INGRES', *IEEE Transactions on Software Engineering*, **SE-5**, 3(May).

17 Thomas, R.H., 1979. 'A majority consensus approach to concurrency control for multiple copy databases', *ACM Transactions on Database Systems*, **4**, 2(June), 180–209.

18 Ullman, J.D., 1982. *Principles of Database Systems* (second edition). Rockville, Maryland: Computer Science Press Inc.
19 Yu, C.T. and Chang, C.C., 1984. 'Distributed Query Processing', *ACM Computing Surveys*, **16**, 4(Dec), 399–433.

CHAPTER SEVEN

PARALLEL PROGRAMMING LANGUAGES

Issues of concurrency have always attracted serious attention in operating systems and other software design. Several techniques including locks, semaphores, monitors, guarded regions and path expressions have been proposed and adopted in order to manage concurrent processing (*see* Andrews and Schneider, 1983).

Some of these techniques have been incorporated into the design of concurrent programming languages. These languages were designed to facilitate the writing of concurrent programs for uniprocessor systems, multiprocessor systems with shared memory and, in some cases, loosely coupled systems. New constructs for interprocess communication and synchronization were introduced into some of these languages.

The increased interest in parallel architectures has generated some activity in the design of parallel languages in order to make the best possible use of these machines. Many of the design issues do not differ fundamentally from those that arose in earlier concurrent language projects. The term 'parallel programming language' is used in this chapter to refer to both the earlier and the more recent projects.

Three major issues are:

(a) What program language construct must be used to specify subtasks (or tasks) which can form parallel streams of activity?
(b) How is it possible to implement a communication mechanism among the subtasks?
(c) How can subtask activity be synchronized in order to ensure correct results at all times?

The process concept is commonly used to refer to some segment of a program that is allocated to a processor. Some parallel languages choose the process as the subtask, and therefore the process is the level at which parallelism is implemented. Other languages group processes together to form larger modules as their subtasks. On the other hand, subtask distribution may occur at the level of single instructions (see Figure 7.1).

Communication is, in some cases, afforded through procedure calling mechanisms. This may involve access to shared data areas for which concurrency control measures have to be employed. Message passing is another technique that has been used. Messages may be buffered in areas outside the name space of the communicating subtasks. In other instances, messages may be unbuffered, in which case it may not be possible to send a message unless someone is ready to receive it.

Synchronization methods include:

(a) explicit wait and signal operations to control access to critical regions;
(b) the evaluation of Boolean expressions to determine whether it is safe to execute some sequence of instructions; and
(c) the use of some message-passing protocol which must precede interprocess communication.

We will look briefly and informally at a number of parallel language projects to acquire some appreciation for the many ways in which these issues have been handled. Since the aim is merely to give the reader a flavour of the proposals and underlying philosophy, details will be omitted.

The study of parallel language design can be divided into the categories: von Neumann-type languages and non von Neumann-type. Among the von Neumann-type, the array processor (or SIMD computer) merits separate discussion. Therefore in the sections that follow, there will be discussions of parallel language design for the array processor, other von Neumann-type parallel language projects, and the non von Neumann class.

7.1 PARALLEL LANGUAGE DESIGN FOR THE ARRAY PROCESSOR (VON NEUMANN)

The ILLIAC IV, operational in a production environment since 1975, is one of the best known array processors (see section 2.4.2). One of the significant results of a survey conducted among ILLIAC IV users in 1979 (Perrott and Stevenson, 1981) was that the high level programming languages had insufficient or inefficient structures thus necessitating the use of machine code.

Users expressed difficulty with, among other things, the organization of data within the processing elements, and with the transfer of data from the backing store to primary store. Users, it seemed, preferred a language

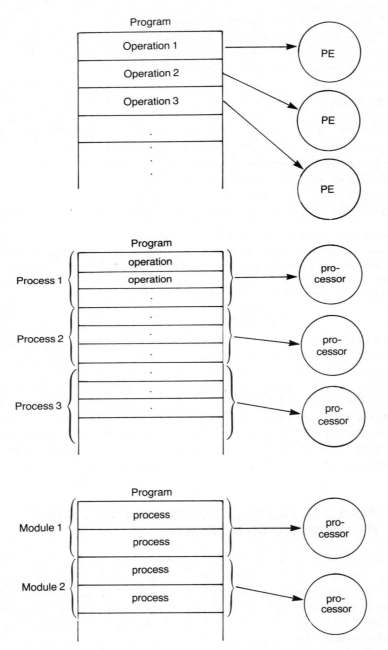

Fig. 7.1   Parallelism can be implemented at different levels of programming

with sufficient abstraction to allow the specification of the parallelism of the problem rather than that of the computer.

Most of the languages used were extensions of languages specifically designed for sequential machines. In an attempt to correct this problem, a parallel language, *Actus*, was designed (Perrott, 1979).

7.1.1 Actus

Perrott outlined several criteria for the design of Actus. These included:

(a) the hiding of the hardware from the user;
(b) the facility to express the parallelism of the problem;
(c) the facility to vary the extent of parallelism;
(d) explicit and data-driven control of parallelism; and
(e) the facility to indicate the minimum working set size of the database.

In Actus, the array is the main data structure for indicating variables that are to be manipulated in parallel. Pascal-like notation is used to describe the features of the language. The maximum extent of parallelism can be declared by using a colon, ':', rather than a pair of sequential dots, '..', in one of the index ranges. For example:

var data: **array**[1:6,   1..6]**of** *real*

indicates that 6 elements of the array 'data' can be manipulated in parallel. These elements will be selected one from each row (see Figure 7.2). The declaration:

var pdata: **array**[1..6,1:4]**of** *real*

indicates that four elements, one from each column, can be manipulated in parallel (see Figure 7.3). The parallelism is restricted to only one dimension at a time. The extent of parallelism is not related to the number of processing elements and, each time a *parallel variable* is used in a

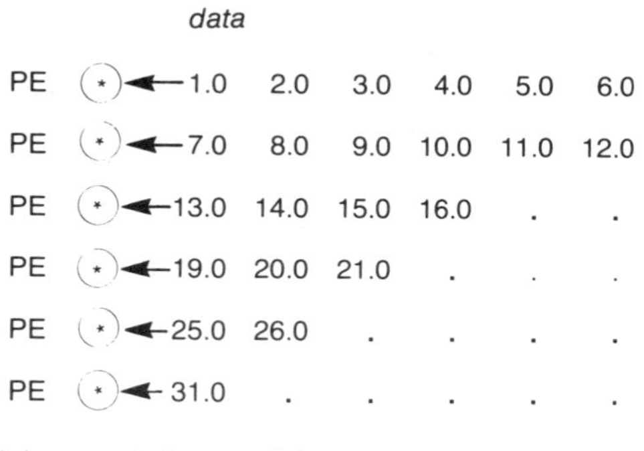

Fig. 7.2   Parallel computation, applying operator * column-wise. One element from each row is selected to form the parallel operand

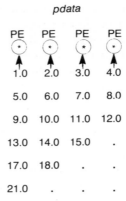

Fig. 7.3 Parallel computation, applying operator *, row-wise. One element from each column is selected to form the parallel operand

statement, its extent of parallelism can be less than or equal to the declared maximum extent of parallelism.

A one-dimensional parallel array of integers can be used as an index of parallel variables whose dimension is greater than one. This allows the parallel manipulation of sets of elements which are not in the same row or column. For example, if 'parindex' is declared as:

$$\textbf{var} \text{ parindex}: \quad \textbf{array}[1:6]\textbf{of } integer$$

then the reference,

$$\text{data}[1:6, \text{parindex}[1:6]]$$

will invoke the parallel manipulation of the 6 elements in rows 1 to 6 with the ith element selected from the column indicated by 'parindex$[i]$' (see Figure 7.4).

Two operators are provided, *shift* and *rotate*, to permit movement of data between elements of the same or different parallel variables. The *shift* enables movement from right to left or from left to right within the extent of parallelism. The *rotate* enables a left or right circular shift within the extent of parallelism.

It was felt that the language should permit many, if not all, of the operations that exist in a sequential environment. Hence facilities were provided to include parallel variables in structured statements like *if*, *case*, *while* and *for*, and in function and procedure declarations. Once the extent of parallelism is defined, the parallel variable can be referenced in any Pascal-like statement.

Another useful facility is that the user can specify the minimum working set size, i.e. the minimum amount of data required to be resident in the fast store in order to permit processing without excessive transfers. The problems handled in these parallel machines sometimes require large volumes of data (e.g. a large matrix), elements of which cannot all be held in the fast store at the same time, hence the need to perform repeated transfers of data between backing store and the fast store.

parindex

4, 5, 3, 1, 2, 1

data [1:6, parindex [1:6]]

1.0   2.0   3.0   (4.0)   5.0   6.0

7.0   8.0   9.0   10.0   (11.0)   .

13.0   14.0   (15.0)   16.0   .   .

(19.0)   20.0   21.0   .   .   .

25.0   (26.0)   27.0   .   .   .

(31.0)   32.0   .   .   .   36.0

Fig. 7.4 With this instance of parindex the circled elements will be operated on in parallel. One element, denoted by the column number parindex [i] is selected from each row to form the parallel operand

Performance levels can be significantly improved if the minimum working set size is known. This information can be used to determine suitable buffer and page sizes for transfer. Actus allows the user to declare this working set size by appending a positive integer to the index that changes most slowly during calculation. For example,

var   work: **array**[1 : 100, 1 . . 50(3)] **of** *real*

indicates a minimum working set size of 100 * 3 = 300 elements.

When implemented on a particular array processor, the variable extents of parallelism declared in the program have to be mapped onto the fixed number of processing elements available in the machine. Where the declared extent is less than the number of processing elements, the extra PEs can be masked (see section 2.4.2). Where an array has a parallel index greater than the number of PEs, the array can be stored in consecutive rows (each row being less than or equal to the number of PEs) with the *i*th element of each row being operated on by the *i*th PE.

Perrott has also discussed ways in which this language can be used on *vector* (pipelined) computers like the Cray-1 and Cray-2 (see section 2.1).

7.2   OTHER VON NEUMANN-TYPE LANGUAGES

In this section we will look at Concurrent Pascal, CSP, DP, PLITS, Ada and SR. However, there are other interesting projects, a partial list of which includes Modula (Wirth, 1979), Edison (Brinch Hansen, 1981), Gypsy (Ambler et al, 1977), Concurrent Euclid (Holt, 1982) and *MOD (Cook, 1980).

7.2.1   Concurrent Pascal

Concurrent Pascal (Brinch Hansen, 1975; 1977) was designed especially to facilitate the writing of operating systems. It is an extension of Pascal with new features permitting the specification of monitors and concurrent processes. The monitor construct is used to handle interprocess communication and synchronization.

The process contains its own private data and a number of statements that are to be executed sequentially. No process has access to the private data of another process. Shared data structures are required for interaction among processes. The shared data structure and the operations (procedures) that can be made on that data structure form a monitor.

Processes can communicate with other processes by calling the procedures within a particular monitor. This results in changes being made to the shared data area. Only one process at a time is allowed access to the monitor, hence monitors also synchronize process activity.

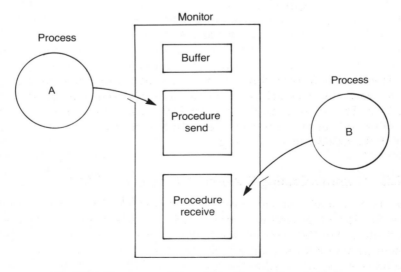

Fig. 7.5   Processes communicate via a monitor structure

For example, assume that process A would like to send a line of text to process B. A buffer to hold that line of text will be shared by the two processes. Process A will send the text to the shared buffer while process B will receive the text from the shared buffer.

The shared buffer and the procedures 'send' and 'receive' will form a monitor (see Figure 7.5). Processes A and B will call the procedures 'send' and 'receive' respectively in order to communicate. Each process has exclusive access to the monitor during the execution of the respective procedures. The programmer should ensure that the procedures are designed to permit receive only from a full buffer, and send only to an empty buffer.

Figure 7.6 provides the code for this buffer example.

```
type   messagebuffer=
monitor
var   contents:   line;
         full:   boolean;
         sender, receiver:   queue;
procedure entry receive (var message:   line);
begin
      if not full then delay (receiver)
      message : = contents; full : = false
      continue (sender);
end;
procedure entry send (message:   line);
begin
      if full then delay (sender);
      contents : = message;   full : = true
      continue (receiver);
end;
begin full : = false end;
```

Fig. 7.6

The monitor forces calling processes to wait by executing the *delay* on a *queue* variable. The delayed process loses its exclusive access to the monitor. This access can only be regained when another process enters the monitor and causes a *continue* operation to be executed on the queue in which the first process is waiting.

7.2.2   Communicating Sequential Processes (CSP)

CSP is a parallel language proposed by Hoare (1978) that permits the specification of programs particularly (but not exclusively) for MIMD machines. MIMD systems have many processors each capable of executing its own program on data obtained from a dedicated memory module (see section 2.4.3).

In CSP, the word 'process' refers to a number of sequential commands which together can be viewed as some subtask or unit of activity. Commands may be simple or structured. Execution of a structured command fails if any one of its constituent commands fails.

A parallel command specifies a number of processes that are to be executed in parallel. All the processes start simultaneously and the parallel command terminates successfully only if and when all the processes have successfully terminated.

Communication between concurrently executing processes is through *input* and *output* commands. Three conditions must hold before communication can take place between two processes. If process A wants to send output to process B, then:

(a) an *input command* in B must specify that A is the source of the input;
(b) an *output* command in A must specify that B is the destination of the output; and
(c) the target variable specified for the receipt of input must match that specified by the *output* command.

When these conditions are satisfied, the *input* and *output* commands are said to correspond and they are executed simultaneously. Hence a process cannot send a message to another unless the destination process is ready to accept it. In this way process activity is synchronized.

For example, let there be two processes 'receive' and 'send' defined as:

$$\text{receive:: send?}(x,y)$$
$$\text{send:: receive! } (a+b,c*3)$$

where the process 'receive' has the *input* command denoted by '?', specifying that a pair of values are to be input from process 'send' and assigned to variables x and y; and the process 'send' has the *output* command!, specifying that the values $a+b, c*3$ are to be output to the process 'receive' (see Figure 7.7). When process 'receive' issues its *input*

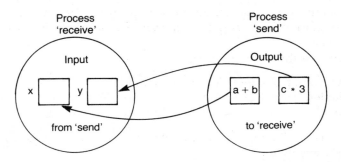

Process
'receive'

Process
'send'

Input

Output

x   [ ] y [ ]   [a + b] [c * 3]

from 'send'   to 'receive'

Fig. 7.7   Input and output are executed simultaneously to effect assignment

command and process 'send' its *output* command, they will be executed simultaneously to produce the effect

$$x := a + b$$
$$y := c * 3$$

where := is the assignment operator.

7.2.3 Distributed Processes (DP)

Brinch Hansen (1978) proposed DP as a language concept for real-time applications controlled by microcomputer networks with distributed storage. Real-time applications need the ability to specify a fixed number of concurrent tasks that can respond quickly to nondeterministic (specific order unknown) requests. Hence the parallel languages should support the following properties:

(a) a fixed number of concurrent processes that are started simultaneously and exist forever, with each process accessing its own variables;
(b) processes can communicate with each other by calling common procedures defined within processes; and
(c) processes are synchronized by means of *guarded regions*.

A *process* has the following format:

process name
own variables
common procedures
initial statement

A process begins execution with its initial statement and continues until the statement either terminates or waits for a condition to be satisfied. The common procedures permit external requests from other processes. Therefore, having executed the initial statement the process may start another operation in response to some external request. When this is terminated, or some waiting is necessary, the process may either resume an earlier operation (if some condition waited for has become true) or start a new operation in response to another external request. This can continue forever.

A *procedure* has the following format:

proc name(input parameters, output parameters)
local variables
statement

A process, *A*, can call a procedure, *C*, defined in another process, *B*, by using a *call* statement, e.g.

call B.C(input param, out param)

For synchronization of process activity, there is the *guarded region* which involves *when* and *cycle* statements. The *when* statement indicates that the process must wait until a particular condition is true before executing some corresponding statement. The *cycle* statement indicates an endless repetition of a *when* statement.

Brinch Hansen has demonstrated how the 'wait' and 'signal' operations on a semaphore initialized to zero can be implemented in DP. Define a process, 'sem', as follows:

```
process sem;   s:   int
proc wait when   s>0:   s:=s−1 end
proc signal;   s:=s+1
s := 0.
```

Other processes can call sem in the following manner:

```
call sem.wait
call sem.signal.
```

7.2.4   Programming language in the sky (PLITS)

PLITS is a programming language (Feldman, 1979) designed for distributed computing. It embodies the concepts of distinct modules and a message passing communication scheme.

The module can be viewed as a selfcontained subtask of a distributed program. Communication among modules is not through shared data areas or shared storage, but instead the names of messages are used for module interaction.

Before modules can communicate, these names must be declared public by all the participating modules, which must all belong to the same job. The message is a pair consisting of its name and its value, where value denotes the information that is to be relayed. Compare this approach with the use of ports discussed in Chapter 4.

For example, if module *A* wants to send a character to module *B*, then module *A* must declare a data area to hold that character, and declare a public name, say '*S*', for it. Similarly, module *B* must declare a data area to receive that character, and declare the same public name '*S*' for naming the message that contains that character (see Figure 7.8).

Furthermore, in order to identify the receiver and sender modules, an additional message pair is needed in each module. This message pair contains its name, e.g. 'who' and a value which is the name of a module, e.g. '*A*' or '*B*' (see Figure 7.8).

An underlying message handling kernel maintains buffers for temporarily holding messages to be delivered later. Module *A* can communicate with *B* by sending the (who, *B*) and (*S*, character) pairs to the kernel, where 'character' is the value of the message. When *B* issues the

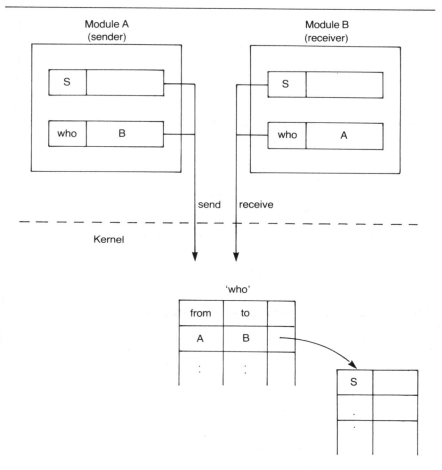

Fig. 7.8 Modules communicate via publicly named message pairs

receive from (who, *A*), the message '*S*', the kernel will put the character into *B*'s data area. On the other hand, *A*'s send request can be issued after *B*'s receive request (see Figure 7.8).

PLITS contains other useful techniques for establishing effective communication protocols.

7.2.5 Ada

In Ada (Pyle, 1981) the parallel strands of activity within a program can each be identified and denoted as a *task*. Tasks can be executed on separate processors or concurrently on a single-processor system.

Tasks are declared within some program unit called its parent. Whenever the parent unit is to be executed, all tasks within it are started and will be executed in parallel unless there are explicit commands to do otherwise.

One task may use services provided by another task within the same parent. Any such service is declared within the server task as an *entry* which can subsequently be called by the other tasks. The server task is delayed until there is a request for service. This delay is implemented through the *accept* statement in the server task. When the server reaches the *accept*, it waits for a request, which is like a procedure call, from the calling task (see Figure 7.9).

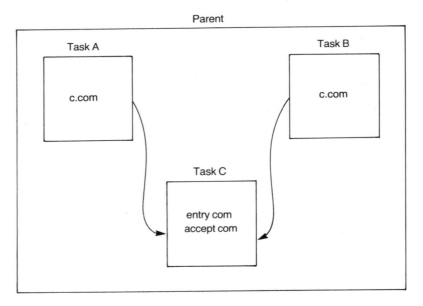

Fig. 7.9   Tasks A and B use the services provided by Task C. Task C waits at 'accept' for entry from calling tasks

This meeting of *call* and *accept* is referred to as a *rendezvous*. The rendezvous action involves execution of the statements indicated by the *accept*. At the end of the rendezvous, the calling task resumes execution and, at the same time, the server task continues execution after the *accept* statement.

The calling task must know the name of the server task and the appropriate entry point, while the server does not have to know who is calling. Therefore, communication is afforded through a known server task which can be viewed as a medium of communication (van den Bos, 1980). The similarity between this construct and the client-server model of distributed computing discussed in section 2.2 and Chapter 5 should be obvious.

```
task CHARACTERBUFFER is
    entry WRITE (CHAR : in CHARACTER); :
    entry READ (CHAR : out CHARACTER);
end CHARACTERBUFFER
task body CHARACTERBUFFER is
    CHARBUFFER : CHARACTER;
begin
    loop
        accept WRITE (CHAR : in CHARACTER) do
            CHARBUFFER := CHAR;
        end WRITE;
        accept READ (CHAR : out CHARACTER) do
            CHAR := CHARBUFFER;
        end READ;
        exit when CHARBUFFER = ASCII.EOF
    end loop
end CHARACTERBUFFER;
task PRODUCER;
task body PRODUCER is
    PROCHAR : CHARACTER;
begin
    loop
        —— produce PROCHAR
        CHARACTERBUFFER.WRITE(PROCHAR);
    end loop;
end PRODUCER;
task CONSUMER;
task body CONSUMER is
    CONCHAR : CHARACTER;
begin
    loop
        CHARACTERBUFFER.READ(CONCHAR);
        —— process CONCHAR
    end loop
end CONSUMER;
```

Fig. 7.10

Figure 7.10 gives a possible Ada implementation of the producer-consumer relationship. The producer writes a character to a buffer, while the consumer reads the character from the buffer.

7.2.6 Synchronizing resources (SR)

SR is proposed by Andrews (1981) as a high level, structured solution to a wide range of parallel programming problems.

In SR, a program includes a number of *resources* which define operations. The word 'resource' is used to express the principle that any facility, whether hardware or software, provides some service that can be tapped. Low level resources can be combined to provide services at higher levels in a hierarchy. A program provides a resource or resources which can be used to achieve some objective.

Each *resource* contains one or more processes in which the operations are implemented. A *resource* also contains variables that are shared among these processes. Processes within the same resource can cooperate through the shared variables. All processes, whether in the same resource or not, can communicate through *operations*.

A process contains its own local variables, to which no other process has access, and a list of statements. These statements may include *operations*. An operation is the vehicle for interprocess communication and synchronization.

The operation is like a procedure. It specifies some number of commands that are to be executed on formal parameters. The execution of the commands may be subject to some Boolean expression being true. Each operation is identified by a name.

Processes invoke an operation by issuing either a *call* or *send* statement which names the particular operation. However, interprocess communication across resources is possible only through operations that are defined as exported or external.

The *call* statement affords synchronous communication in that the calling process is delayed until the process that owns the operation executes it. The *send* statement affords asynchronous communication in that the invoking process may proceed as soon as the actual parameter values have been transmitted.

For example, if process *A* would like to send a message to process *B*, a send operation must be defined and named in some process *C*, to accept a character string from a formal parameter and deposit the character string at another formal parameter. Similarly, a receive operation must be defined and named. Furthermore, these operations should be declared external if use by processes in other resources is anticipated.

Now process *A* can invoke the send operation (through a *call* or a *send*) by naming the operation and providing actual parameters for the location and the value of the message. Similarly, process *B* can invoke the receive operation. These operations are uniquely identified by the name which includes resource, process and operation name.

A possible SR implementation of the producer-consumer relationship, with the buffer having a bound of 10 slots, is given in Figure 7.11.

This solution allows concurrent execution of the *produce* and *consume* operations since they are in different processes. An underlying assumption is that references to the shared variables are atomic. Producers and consumers can use this communication resource by calling *produce* and *consume* respectively.

7.3 SYSTEMS PROGRAMMING WITH C

It should be clear from our look at these parallel languages that the aim is to facilitate the implementation of distributed systems by providing high

```
resource boundedbuffer;
    define produce, consume {call}
    var buffer: array [0. .9] of message;
        slots, messages: integer;
    slots := 10; messages := 0
    process put;
        do true →
            in produce(m: message) and (slots-messages) > 0 →'
                buffer [messages mod 10]: = m;
                messages := messages + 1
            ni
        od
    end put
    process get;
        do true →
            in consume(var m: message)
                    and (slots-messages) < 10 →
                m := buffer [slots mod 10];
                slots := slots + 1
            ni
        od
    end get
end boundedbuffer
```

Fig. 7.11

level language constructs. The programmer is allowed to operate more at the particular problem level than at the machine level.

However, most of these languages are not widely available and, furthermore, they do not provide the sort of low level control that is sometimes needed by the systems programmer in order to develop efficient operating systems for distributed environments. It follows, therefore, that the systems programmer must still code in a low-level language in order to manipulate registers, to perform operations on bit level fields, and to control synchronous and asynchronous activity among the hardware units.

It is in this regard that we will look briefly at a systems programming language that has provided the opportunity to handle programming tasks that formerly would have demanded a great deal of skill in assembly language coding. That language is C. It is not a parallel language but it is, nonetheless, quite useful for the machine-oriented coding required at the lower level of systems implementation. It allows low level control while providing the programmer with the facility to use high level constructs. As a result of its versatility, C is becoming increasingly popular among systems programmers.

The C programming language

The C programming language was designed and developed by Dennis Ritchie at Bell Laboratories (Kernighan and Ritchie, 1978) as a systems programming language for the UNIX operating system. It has been acclaimed for its facilities for controlling the hardware at a low level and for building high level data and control structures.

There are four basic data types in C. These are:

(a) *char* – a character which is internally represented as a single byte;
(b) *int* – an integer which is stored as one word of the host machine;
(c) *float* – a single precision floating point number;
(d) *double* – a double precision floating point number.

The 'string' is not a basic data type, but can be formed as an array of type *char*. Unlike most other languages, C permits arithmetic on characters, as well as logical comparisons with other characters or integers.

C supports pointers which can be incremented without programmer knowledge of the exact physical width of the elements pointed to. This facility provides hardware independence. The programmer need only specify the type of the data item being pointed to. For example, if p points to an object of size x bytes, then $p + 1$ points to the 'next' occurrence of the object, i.e. the length in bytes, x is added to the integer value of p.

There are declarations which can be used in order to have some control over the allocation of storage. Among these are:

(a) the *register* qualifier which, when used, is a request that the data should be stored in a machine register; and
(b) the *auto* qualifier which requests automatic storage allocation: variable storage within a block is automatically allocated when that block is entered and deallocated upon exit.

C provides facilities for the building of data structures using any set of legal C data types. Furthermore, via the *'typeof'* declaration, a user can form his or her own type and, via the *union*, a user can view one storage area in more than one way.

In addition to the usual arithmetic, logical and other operators, C provides some unconventional ones. For incrementing and decrementing there are $++$ and $--$ respectively, which can be applied to a variable within an expression. The effect is to increment/decrement that variable before or after computation of the expression. For example:

$$y = (++x) + 6$$

increments x before computing y; and

$$y = (x++) + 6$$

increments x after computing y.

Assignment operations like

$$x = x + y$$

can be written as

$$x + = y.$$

Other operators, e.g. $-$, $*$, can be used in this way. C also permits the explicit conversion of a variable from one type to another.

C allows the use of control structures like *if, for, while, do-while,* and *switch.* The *switch* has the following form:

```
switch (expression)
{
case constant 1:
        statement set 1
case constant 2:
        statement set 2

        .

        .

        .

default:
        statement set n
}
```

It permits the execution of a certain statement set from a range of statement sets if a constant associated with that statement set is equal to a value derived from a specified expression. However, execution will continue through the other cases unless there is a *break* statement which takes you out of the switch. Other control statements are *continue* and *goto* (with statement labels).

Biggerstaff (1986) has presented an introduction to C and a number of software routines written in that language for many systems programming tasks including the handling of communications hardware. The interested reader is encouraged to refer to his *Systems Software Tools.*

7.4 NON VON NEUMANN-TYPE LANGUAGES

Non von Neumann-type languages constitute a fundamentally different approach to parallel programming. As we have seen in Chapter 2, the principles of data flow and functional programming facilitate parallelism down to the single operation level.

Functional programming languages employ the mathematical concept of a function as the basic language construct (Henderson, 1980). For example, the mathematical notation $f(x)$ is used, and interpreted as the result obtained after applying the function f to some object, x. The term *applicative language* is often used to refer to such a language.

A program can be expressed as a functional form involving the combination of defined functions at several levels of a hierarchy. Functions operate only on their arguments. As long as the function is known and the arguments are available, the result can be computed. The particular characteristics of the program will determine how many functions can be executed in parallel.

Data-flow programs are based on the principle that operations can be performed as long as the operands are available. They are traditionally expressed as *directed graphs* with the nodes representing the operations and the arcs the flow of data. Textual languages with a functional style have been designed to reflect the features of data flow. The nodes in a data flow graph can be mapped onto separate processing elements.

Unlike von Neumann languages, these languages do not possess the concept of variables which are used to name memory locations to and from which data are written and read. Instead, computation involves the manipulation of objects, hence the term *variable-free language* is often used.

In fact, Turner's (1979) implementation technique for applicative languages removes the variables altogether. He uses results from combinatory logic to replace the applicative functions by variable-free identities. This resulting code can be efficiently executed by a simple machine called the S-K reduction machine.

For example, given a definition typically expressed as

$$\textbf{def} \quad f\,x = \ldots$$

where '. . .' is some expression involving the variable x, the system obtains a form free of that variable x. If

$$x + 1$$

can be written as:

$$\textbf{plus } 1\,x$$

i.e. apply the function 'plus 1' to x, then the definition

$$\textbf{def suc } x = x + 1$$

can be expressed as:

$$\textbf{def suc } x = \textbf{plus } 1\,x$$

which, when the variable x is removed, becomes

$$\textbf{def suc } = \textbf{plus } 1.$$

Turner uses combinators (i.e. combinations of functions are given named definitions) to facilitate the removal of the variable in the general case. Three of those combinators are **S**, **K** and **I** which are defined as:

$$\textbf{S}\,f\,g\,x = f\,x\,(g\,x)$$
$$\textbf{K}\,x\,y = x$$
$$\textbf{I}\,x = x.$$

The first two appear in the name of his reduction machine.

Some of the most notable functional languages are Lisp (McCarthy, 1962), FP (Backus, 1978), LUCID (Ashcroft and Wadge, 1977), SASL (Turner, 1979); while pioneering work on data flow by Dennis (1974) has been followed by (among others) ID (Arvind et al, 1978), Val (Ackerman and Dennis, 1979) and CAJOLE (Hankin and Glaser, 1981).

Some of these languages have been implemented on von Neumann machines in environments where other types of machines are unavailable. In other cases, the language design project is a part of a larger project which includes design of a data flow or reduction machine (see section 2.5).

We will look briefly and informally at some of these languages.

7.4.1 Functional Programming (FP)

FP was designed by Backus (1978) as a programming system in which programs are simply functions without variables. Functions map objects into objects and always take a single argument. New functions can be built from existing functions by employing a fixed set of combining forms called functional forms.

There is only one operation in FP. It is called *application*, e.g. $f:x$ is an application which denotes the object obtained when function f is applied to x.

There are basic primitive functions which can be used to build higher level functional forms. These primitive functions include *Identity, Equals, Add, Subtract* and other useful fundamental operations. For example, the primitive function $+:x$, where x is a sequence of numbers $<x1, x2>$, when applied would return the result $x1 + x2$.

Several functional forms are defined using other functions or objects as parameters. For example, $f{\circ}g$ is the *composition* of f and g.

$(f{\circ}g):x = f:(g:x)$ implies that g is applied to x, following which f is applied to the result.

Symbolic function names can be given to functional forms by using a *definition* statement. For example if,

Def ans$*0[+,-]$, where $*$ is the multiply operator, then if we apply ans to $<4,2>$, the following steps will be taken

$$\text{ans} => (*_0[+,-]):<4,2>$$
$$=> *_0[+,-]:<4,2>$$
$$=> * :<+:<4,2>,-:<4,2>>$$
$$=> * :<6,2>$$
$$=> \ 12.$$

Parallelism can be implemented by identifying the inherently parallel *application* operators and allocating them to distinct processing elements.

7.4.2   Lisp and Multilisp

Lisp is a functional style language catering for the manipulation of symbolic expressions. A symbolic expression is either an *atom* – a string of characters of indefinite length regarded as a whole item – or a list of elements enclosed in parentheses where the element may be an atom, a list of atoms or even a list of lists. Hence list can be recursively defined.

For example, a, b, c, abc are four atoms, and

$$
\begin{array}{l}
\text{(a b c abc)} \\
\text{(a (b c abc))} \\
\text{((a b) (c abc))}
\end{array}
$$

are lists.

Elementary functions are provided for fundamental operations on symbolic expressions, e.g. the function *car* extracts the first element of a list. Church's (1941) lambda calculus is used to facilitate the specification of procedures as functions and the application of these functions to their arguments.

For example,

$$(\text{name } (lambda \ (xyz) \ (\text{car } xyz)))$$

is a lambda expression called 'name', which defines a function that takes a list as argument and applies the elementary function *car* to that list. Subsequent references to 'name' with any list as argument will return the first character of that list. Lisp also permits recursive definition of functions.

There are many different Lisp systems embodying this fundamental functional approach. Multilisp (Halstead, 1985) is a version of Lisp that includes constructs for explicitly requesting parallel execution.

The objects that are manipulated by Multilisp tasks reside in one shared name space. Therefore Multilisp is suitable for a shared memory parallel computer.

The principal constructs for parallel execution in Multilisp are *pcall* and *future*. Parallel execution of the expressions which form the arguments of a function can be obtained if *pcall* is used in the reference to that function, e.g.,

$$(pcall \text{ func arga argb})$$

specifies concurrent evaluation of 'arga' and 'argb'. In this construct, the application of the function 'func' to the arguments will follow the evaluation of the expressions that are the arguments.

However, the evaluation of the 'func' may involve the creation of some data structure which can be done before the results from evaluating 'arga' and 'argb' are available. It is useful, therefore, to let the building of the data structure proceed in parallel with the evaluation of the arguments.

This can be obtained by using the *future* construct, e.g.,

$$(\text{func } (future \text{ arga}) (future \text{ argb})).$$

Hence Multilisp allows the programmer explicit specification of parallelism in a manner that conforms with the normal syntax of the language.

7.4.3 CAJOLE

CAJOLE is a textual data flow programming language (Hankin and Glaser, 1981). The sequencing of instructions in the data flow environment is controlled by the data dependencies between operations. These dependencies are usually expressed in a directed graph (see Figure 2.11) where the nodes represent the operations and the arcs show the flow of data. CAJOLE reflects this philosophy.

A CAJOLE program is a list of function definitions which may be presented in any order. A function definition has the form

$$yplusz = [y,z]y+z$$

where 'yplusz' is the name of the function, the bracketed list contains the formal parameters and '$y + z$' defines the value of the function. Functions can be defined recursively.

Function application is invoked by using the name of the function, with actual parameters as arguments, in another definition, e.g.

$$a = yplusz \ (b, c).$$

These textual higher-level definitions are supported by a number of underlying primitive operators which form the lower-level language and are used to construct the directed graph of the program.

The implementation proposal incorporates a *librarian* for holding function definitions, and an *evaluator* for executing the primitive operations. The *librarian*, upon request, will associate actual values with the formal parameters of named functions, and generate a function graph with the appropriate data on its input arcs. The *evaluator* will then execute the function.

7.5 SUMMARY

Parallel programming languages facilitate the writing of concurrent programs. These languages allow the specification of different parallel streams of activity within a program. They also provide mechanisms for interaction among these parallel tasks.

Parallel languages can be classified broadly as either von Neumann-type or non von Neumann. The von Neumann-type contains examples of sequential languages to which parallel features have been added. However, there are projects which are designed specifically for parallel programming.

The tasks for concurrent execution in the von Neumann languages range from single processes to collections of processes called modules or resources. Tasks communicate with each other either through procedure call or message-passing mechanisms.

Task activity can be synchronized by regulating access to shared data and procedures or by ensuring that some protocol be followed before communication can take place.

Where it is required to obtain greater hardware control it may still be necessary to code in assembly language. The C programming language has reduced this need to program at such a low level. It provides hardware level control using relatively high-level structures. Although not a parallel language, it is useful for the implementation of the machine-oriented aspects of distributed systems software.

Functional and data flow languages permit a departure from von Neumann architecture and create possibilities for parallelism down to the level of single operations.

7.6 QUESTIONS

7.1 Assume that you had to multiply the 10*8 array A by a scalar S. How would you specify in Actus that the operation on the array elements is to be done in parallel?

7.2 How is interprocess activity synchronized in Concurrent Pascal?

7.3 In what way is the communication system in CSP suitable for a MIMD computer?

7.4 In what ways does Brinch Hansen's DP differ from his Concurrent Pascal?

7.5 Indicate the differences between a message passing system and a procedure call system.

7.6 Compare message passing in PLITS with the use of ports in Accent (see section 4.2.3).

7.7 In what way is interprocess communication in Ada similar to a client-server distributed model?

7.8 SR permits both procedure call and message passing communication mechanisms. How is this done?

7.9 Explain the use of the term 'functional programming language'.

7.10 How can a functional programming language facilitate parallelism in the execution of instructions?

7.11 Indicate any differences or similarities observed between FP and Lisp.

7.12 What is the purpose of the librarian in CAJOLE?

7.13 What would you say is the significance of Turner's implementation technique?

7.14 Indicate some of the features of the C programming language that make it suitable for systems programming.

7.7 REFERENCES

1 Ackerman, W.B., and Dennis, J.B., 1979. *VAL: A value oriented algorithmic language, preliminary reference manual.* Technical Report TR-218, Lab for Computer Science, MIT.

2 Ambler, A.L. et al, 1977. 'Gypsy: a language for specification and implementation of verifiable programs', *ACM Sigplan Notices*, **12**, 3, 1–10.

3 Andrews, G.R., 1981. 'Synchronizing Resources', *ACM Transactions on Programming Languages & Systems*, **3**, 4, 405–431.

4 Andrews, G.R. and Schneider, F.B., 1983. 'Concepts and notations for concurrent processing', *ACM Computing Surveys*, **15**, 1, 3–44.

5 Arvind, Gostelow, K.P. and Plouffe, W., 1978. *An asynchronous programming language and computing machine.* Technical Report 114a, Department of Information and Computer Science, Irvine, University of California.

6 Ashcroft, E.A. and Wadge, W.W., 1977. 'LUCID, a nonprocedural language with iteration', *Communications of the ACM*, **20**, 7, 519–526.

7 Backus, J., 1978. 'Can programming be liberated from the von Neumann style? A functional style and its algebra of programs', *Communications of the ACM*, **21**, 8, 613–641.

8 Biggerstaff, T.J., 1986. *Systems Software Tools.* Englewood Cliffs: Prentice Hall Inc.

9 Brinch Hansen, P., 1975. 'The programming language Concurrent Pascal', *IEEE Transactions Software Engineering*, **1**, 2, 199–207.

10 Brinch Hansen, P., 1977. *The Architecture of Concurrent Programs.* Englewood Cliffs: Prentice Hall Inc.

11 Brinch Hansen, P., 1978. 'Distributed Processes: A concurrent programming concept', *Communications of the ACM*, **21**, 11, 934–940.

12 Brinch Hansen, P., 1981. 'Edison: A multiprocessor language', *Software: Practice and Experience*, **11**, 4, 325–361.

13 Church, A., 1941. *The Calculi of Lambda-Conversion.* Princeton: Princeton University Press.

14 Cook, R.P., 1980. 'MOD: A language for Distributed Computing', *IEEE Transactions on Software Engineering*, **6**, 6, 563–571.

15 Dennis, J.B., 1974. 'First version of a data flow procedure language', in *Lecture notes in Computer Science*, 362–376, **19**, (ed. B. Robinet). New York: Springer-Verlag.

16 Feldman, J.A., 1979. 'High level programming for distributed computing', *Communications of the ACM*, **22**, 6, 353–368.

17 Halstead Jr., R.H., 1985. 'Multilisp: A language for Concurrent Symbolic

Computation', *ACM Transactions on Programming Languages and Systems*, **7**, 4, 501–538.

18 Hankin, C.L. and Glaser, H.W., 1981. 'The data flow programming language CAJOLE: An informal introduction', *ACM Sigplan Notices*, **16**, 7, 35–44.

19 Henderson, P., 1980. *Functional Programming, Application and Implementation*, London: Prentice Hall.

20 Hoare, C.A.R., 1978. 'Communicating Sequential Processes', *Communications of the ACM*, **21**, 8, 666–677.

21 Holt, R.C., 1982. 'A short introduction to Concurrent Euclid', *ACM Sigplan Notices*, **17**, 5, 60–79.

22 Kernighan, B.W. and Ritchie, D.M., 1978. *The C Programming Language*. Englewood Cliffs: Prentice Hall Inc.

23 McCarthy, J. et al, 1962. *LISP 1.5 Programmer's Manual*. Cambridge MIT Press.

24 Perrott, R.H., 1979. 'A language for array and vector processors', *ACM Transactions on Programming Languages & Systems*, **1**, 2, 177–195.

25 Perrott, R.H. and Stevenson, D.K., 1981. 'Users' experiences with the ILLIAC IV system and its programming languages', *ACM Sigplan Notices*, **16**, 7, 75–88.

26 Pyle, I.C., 1981. *The Ada Programming Language*. London: Prentice Hall International.

27 Turner, D.A., 1979. 'A new implementation technique for applicative languages', *Software: Practice and Experience*, **9**, 31–49.

28 van den Bos, J., 1980. 'Comments on Ada process communication', *ACM Sigplan Notices*, **15**, 6, 77–81.

29 Wirth, N., 1979. 'Design and implementation of Modula', *Software: Practice and Experience*, **7**, 67–84.

GLOSSARY

Access method   The manner in which a communication channel is allocated to a computer which has information to transmit.

Agent process   The process that serves as an interface between a local operating system and the computer network.

ALOHA   The first broadcast radio network. It was developed at the University of Hawaii in the early 1970s.

Amplitude Modulation – AM   A technique which employs changes in the amplitude of analog waves to represent digital signals.

Analog wave   A wave that has a continuous form. This differs from digital waves which are not continuous.

Applicative language   A language which allows a functional form where defined functions are applied to objects.

ARPA   Advanced Research Projects Agency of the U.S. Department of Defense; now known as DARPA.

ARPANET   A pioneering network built by DARPA. It is now one of the best known wide area networks.

Array processor   A computer which contains many processing elements which simultaneously perform the same operation on separate data items.

Associative memory   A memory that allows simultaneous access to the same bit position in a number of words.

Associative processor   Enables simultaneous access to an associative memory.

Asynchronous   The characteristic of not being regulated by some set time interval, nor determined by the timing of some other activity.

Atomic transaction   A transaction that either succeeds or has no effect.

Attenuation   The distortion that a wave undergoes after some time interval.

Attribute   A measurable characteristic of an object. For example the name, price or quantity of an item.

Back-off   To stop the activity in which one is presently engaged.

Back-out   To remove the effect of an aborted transaction.

Bandwidth   The range of frequencies that a channel can accommodate.

Baseband signaling   To transmit digital signals without modulation.

Batch   An accumulation of items for some processing function.

Batch processing/stream operation To handle batches in the processing functions.

Baud rate The number of times the signal changes in one second.

Bit stuffing A system of adding redundant bits to a bit stream to preserve the uniqueness of some code.

Block The smallest physical extent of data transferred between the disk and primary store.

Bridge A processor that is dedicated to act as the communications interface between two local networks.

Broadband bus A bus network that allows modulation of the digital signal onto different frequency bands.

Broadband signaling A transmission technique that allows the use of different frequency bands on the same communications medium.

Broadcast A signaling technique where a message can be received by a group of recipients at the same time.

Bus A network system where all the nodes are attached to a single cable which permits transmissions in both directions.

Cambridge ring A ring network developed at Cambridge University.

Capability A name administered by the system and allocated to users for controlled access to objects. The user must supply this name in all attempts to access the associated object. See object model.

CCITT An international organization that administrates standards for telecommunications. CCITT is the abbreviation for Comité Consultatif Internationale de Télégraphique et Téléphonique.

Centralized lock controller A central node that handles all the locks in a distributed system.

Channel A communication path.

Channel capacity The amount of information that a channel can carry.

Checksum A data field usually at the end of a block of data that facilitates the detection of errors that are in the block.

Ciphertext The coded information transmitted in a cryptographic system.

Circuit switching A communication environment in which a complete end-to-end channel is allocated for the duration of a communication session.

Client The software module that resides at user machines and serve as the interface with some server in the client-server distributed system.

Client-server model A service is owned by a particular machine at which a server administers that service. Clients run on the user machines and facilitate user consumption of that service.

Command interpreter/processor The program modules which interpret the commands users make to the operating system.

Command language The vehicle used to build the interface between the user and the operating system. It provides commands that users can issue to the operating system.

Commit An indication that a change to a data area is to be made permanent.

Commit point The point after which a change will be considered permanent.

Communication channel See channel.

Communication link The physical link that accommodates the channels for information exchange.

Communication network   The network of nodes and physical links that make communication among the nodes possible.

Communication processor   A network node that is dedicated to communication functions.

Communication subnet   A network of communication processors.

Computer network   A system of computers linked in a communications network.

Concentrator   A device that takes several input lines and outputs onto a single line.

Concurrency   The facility to accommodate many of the same type of activity at the same time. For example, a number of transactions may access the same file at the same time.

Consistency   All the copies of data areas reflect the same state.

Context-switching   The working environment of a processor is changed to begin execution on another process.

CRC – cyclic redundancy code   A checksum computed using a generator polynomial as divisor and a polynomial representation of the message as dividend.

Cryptography   A system for transmitting encoded information.

CSMA   Carrier sense multiple access. An access method where stations listen to the channel before transmitting.

CSMA/CD   Carrier sense multiple access with collision detection. Stations listen and back-off if they detect a collision.

Cube network   An n-dimensional network of 2^n nodes and each node is linked to n other nodes. The links are determined from a particular routing function.

Database   The central storage of operational data for an organization.

Data-driven   The availability of data triggers some operation on that data.

Data-flow   The movement of data through processing nodes.

Data-flow computer/machine   A computer that is based on the data-flow principle.

Datagram   A packet that belongs to a message and is transmitted independently of the other packets in that message.

Data independence   A characteristic of database systems where the logical relationship among the data items stored is not affected by the changes in the physical organization.

Data integrity   The data items that are manipulated always give a faithful representation of the domain that is being depicted.

DCE   Data communication equipment. The communication processor in X.25 terminology.

Deadlock   A situation where two or more processes/transactions are each waiting on resources that another has and cannot release.

Decibel (dB)   The name given to a measurement of noise levels.

Decrypt   To decode a message that was transmitted by some cryptographic system.

Demand-driven   The reference to a function name demands its application to some object.

Demodulation   The conversion of the analog signal back to a digital form.

Dictionary   A data area that provides a correspondence between names and some other property.

Digital signaling   The transmission system maps the digital values onto discrete voltage levels. There is no modulation.

Directed graph   A graph in which there is direction of flow associated with the arcs.

Directory locator   A data area that provides the address of a directory.

Distributed   The property of being divided up among several sites.

Distributed database system   A collection of cooperating database systems each at a separate site.

Distributed operating system   A homogeneous operating system that is implemented as a set of cooperating operating systems each at a separate site.

DNA   Digital Network Architecture of Digital Equipment Corporation.

Domain   A set of members determined by some prescribed condition each member must satisfy. In a relational database the domain of a relation is the set from which attribute values are selected.

Domain calculus   A system for query processing with the use of domain variables.

Domain variable   A variable that can have a value which belongs to a specified domain.

Down-load   To load from a server machine to a client machine.

DTE   Data terminal equipment. The device that interfaces between the host and the X.25 link, e.g. the host computer.

Electronic funds transfer   The facility to undertake monetary transactions through a computer network.

Electronic mail   The exchange of messages via a computer network.

Empty slot   A facility for allocating a time interval to stations on a network. If the slot is empty it is available.

Encryption   The system of transmitting or storing information in a coded form.

Entity   The word used in database technology to refer to data objects that can be measured.

Entity occurrence   An instance of an entity denoted by a unique set of attributes.

Equijoin   The operation of joining two relations based on equality over some attribute.

Error-correcting code   A data field that provides enough information both to spot an error and derive the correct form.

Error-detecting code   A data field that provides information to detect an error.

Exchange   A data area that serves as intermediary storage for messages in transit.

Fail-soft operation   An environment where failures are not catastrophic.

FDM (frequency division multiplexing)   A mechanism for dividing a wide bandwidth channel into many narrow bandwidth channels for simultaneous use.

File map   A data table that contains entries associating file pages with disk blocks.

File server   A server system that provides some level of file management and storage.

File-store   The physical medium used for storing files.

File transfer   The transmission of a file from one location to another in a network.

Frame   A string of bits enclosed within a begin-frame and an end-frame indicator.

Frame check sequence (FCS)   The checksum field that is appended to a frame.

Frame level control (FLC) The field that contains control information on the frame.

Frequency The number of complete waveforms that are generated in a second. This is referred to as the number of cycles per second and is expressed as Hz (Hertz).

Frequency shift keying (FSK) A modulation technique that maps the digital values onto different frequencies.

Full-duplex Information can travel in both directions at the same time.

Functional language A language that allows the specification of computer programs as combinations of functions.

Functional programming The system of designing and writing computer programs by using a functional language.

Gateway A communications processor that links two networks.

Generator polynomial The polynomial used as the modulo 2 divisor in the generation of the cyclic redundancy code.

Go-Back-N ARQ A communication protocol where there is a window size indicating the number of messages that can be transmitted before waiting for an acknowledgment. ARQ denotes automatic repeat request. After sending messages up to the window size, there is a wait for acknowledgment. All the messages that are not acknowledged within a time-out interval are repeated.

Guarded region A synchronization structure which involves a shared data area that cannot be entered before some boolean variable is true.

Half-duplex Information can be transmitted in both directions but only one direction at a time.

Half-gateway A system where two communications processors, called half-gateways, are dedicated to the link between two networks. Each communication processor interfaces with one network and the other communication processor.

HDLC High-level data link control. The data link protocol of the OSI model.

Hertz (Hz) *See* frequency.

Hierarchical model A structure that embodies a layered system.

Horizontal partitioning A distribution of a relation in a database where the subsets are some of the tuples with all their attributes.

Host A computer in the network that runs the user applications.

Idempotent The property where repetition always produces the same effect as the original.

IMP (Interface Message Processor) This term can be applied to the communications node in a network.

Indefinite postponement The inability to seize a resource when it becomes available. Someone always seem to get there before you.

Indeterminacy The principle of not being able to prescribe any schedule.

Intentions log A record of the individual phases in a transaction in order to determine subsequent action in maintaining a recoverable system.

Interactive The characteristic of being able to monitor and modify a programming sequence during the process of execution.

Inverted list model   A database structure that embodies a set of secondary indexes.

ISO   International Standards Organization.

Kbps   Kilo bits per second, where 1 K is 1024.

Kernel   The part of the operating system that handles the lower level process scheduling etc. It is always resident in primary storage.

Key   A data item that is used to identify a logical collection of data items, or a bit sequence used to drive an encryption algorithm.

LAN (Local area network)   This covers a small area like a building.

Linked list   A data structure where each entry contains a pointer to the next entry. The last entry has a null pointer.

Location transparency   The characteristic of being able to function without knowledge of where the resources used are located.

Lock   A software mechanism that can prevent access to a shared resource.

Log file   A register of activities maintained to facilitate auditing and recovery.

Long-haul network   A network that covers a wide geographical area such as a country.

Loosely coupled system   A multicomputer system where processors have their own main memories.

Mail server   A software system that belongs to the client-server model. It allows users on the client machines to exchange mail.

Majority consensus   An update mechanism in a distributed system where the majority decision on which update to execute is carried.

Mask   To temporarily disable some functional device.

Massively parallel system   A multiprocessor system with thousands of processing elements.

Mbps   Mega (1 million) bits per second.

Mesh   A point-to-point network with some redundant links, and possibly fully connected.

Message passing   An interprocess communication scheme that incorporates explicit send and receive functions with no waiting.

Message switching   A transmission scheme which allocates the communication path in segments. At no time is a complete end-to-end path dedicated.

mHz (mega Hertz: million cycles per second)   *See* frequency.

MIMD (Multiple instruction multiple data stream computer)   The processing elements can execute separate code sequences on separate data areas simultaneously.

Modem (Modulator/demodulator)   A device used in the conversion of digital signals to analog form and vice versa.

Monitor   A synchronization data structure implemented in software to control the access to shared variables and procedures.

Multicomputer systems   A system of more than one computer linked by a high-speed communications network and occupying a small area like a single room.

Multidrop line   A cable that links several terminals to a computer.

Multiplexing   The technique that allows the sharing of a single channel by several stations.

Multiplexor   A device that implements multiplexing.

Multiprocessor   A computer with more than one processor sharing a global memory bank.

Name server   A client-server system that provides resource naming and location services.

Natural language   A language that accommodates the natural speech forms that we use.

Nearest neighbor mesh (NNM)   A network where the nodes are interconnected to their nearest neighboring nodes.

Network model   A database architecture that accommodates any inherent relationship among the entities.

Network operating system   A system of heterogeneous operating systems co-operating through agent processes in a computer network.

Network transparency   The facility of being able to use the services of a computer network without being aware that the network exists.

Node   A processing unit that is linked into a communications network.

Normalization   The process of developing relations which possess certain desirable properties.

Nyquist's theorem   A fundamental theorem in communications that associates the maximum data rate of a channel with the bandwidth and discrete signal values.

Object model   A software system that is built on the principle that all resources can be classified as objects, access to which can be controlled by the system. The system maintains capabilities to these objects, and the user must be given a capability to be used in all accesses to that object. (*See* capability.)

On-line   A physical channel exists facilitating immediate information exchange.

Optical fibers   Transmission media that convey light signals.

OSI   Open systems interconnection.

PABX   Public automatic branch exchange. A switching system which can handle both voice and data communication in a local network.

Packet   A fixed length string of bits which is usually the smallest extent of information transmitted in the network.

Packet switching   Messages are divided into fixed length packets and each packet is transmitted independently one hop at a time. An entire end-to-end path is not dedicated. (*See* message switching.)

Packet Switch Node (PSN)   The communications processor in a packet switching communications subnet.

Page   A fixed number of bytes that can be individually addressed and manipulated. It is often used to support virtual memory systems.

Page map   A data table that associates pages in a file with their location in storage.

Parallel architecture   An architecture that supports parallel processing.

Parallel programming language   A language that allows the specification and manipulation of parallel streams in a program.

Parallel variable   A variable that represents some set of elements that can be operated on in parallel.

Partition failure   A failure that causes some component of the distributed system to be cut off from the remainder.

Partitioning   The division of a distributed database system into distinct parts for separate storage.

Period   The number of seconds taken by a wave to complete one cycle.

Periodic   A wave that repeats its shape with time.

Peripheral processor   A processing unit that controls an I/O device.

Petal   One ring component in a multiring LAN.

Phase change   A difference in angular measure between waves of the same shape.

Phase modulation (PM)   A modulation technique that represents the digital values by phase changes.

Pipeline machine/processor   A computer that begins execution of an instruction before the completion of the previous instruction.

Plaintext   Information that has not been coded.

Plex model   Same as network model.

Point-to-point network   A network in which stations have direct links to other stations. There is no broadcast capability.

Polling   A mechanism used to determine whether stations have information to transmit.

Polynomial code   *See* CRC.

Port   A mechanism used to receive inputs or messages. It can be viewed as an address at which messages can be delivered for the owner of the port.

Primary key   The unique identifier of a record.

Primary node/site   The node or site at which updates are performed immediately in a distributed system. All other copies are updated later.

Primitive operation   The lowest level of operation that can be performed in the given environment.

Printer server   A software system that belongs to the client-server model. It allows users on client machines access to a common printer.

Procedure call   The facility to start execution of another procedure by naming that procedure. The caller waits until the called procedure completes and returns control.

Processing element (PE)   A device that can perform some operation(s) in response to the activation of a stored program.

Protocol   The specifications which when followed make communication among similar objects possible.

Pure aloha   A channel access mechanism in which stations transmit whenever they have packets to send.

Query language   A language which allows the user to make requests to a database system.

Query processing   The handling of the user requests that are made to the database system.

Range variable   A variable that can assume any value from some specified set of values. The variable is said to range over that set.

Real time system   A processing system that provides immediate responses to queries.

Record   The set of data items which describes some entity.

Reduction machine/computer   A computer that supports the principle of progressively reducing functions until some irreducible form is derived.

Register insertion An access method used in ring LANs where a shift register forms part of the interface between the station and the ring.

Relation A two-dimensional structure of entity occurrences and their attributes.

Relational algebra A vehicle for specifying the procedures needed to process queries.

Relational calculus A vehicle for prescribing the conditions that must be satisfied in meeting queries.

Relational model A system that embodies the relation as the basic data structure.

Remote procedure call (RPC) A procedure call mechanism that extends to remote sites. (*See* procedure call.)

Repeater A device that strengthens (repeats) a signal.

Replication To hold a copy of a file at another site.

Roll-back To undo the effect of a transaction.

Root directory The global parent node in a tree-structured directory system.

Root of file The page that contains the header and the page map of the file.

SDLC (Synchronous data link control) A data link protocol used by IBM.

Secondary key An attribute that is not unique to a record. It is used to identify groups of records.

Semijoin A variant of the join operator that is used to reduce the communication cost.

Serializability The scheduling of transactions so that their execution will produce the same effect as if they were performed serially.

Server The software module that manages a service and is located at the machine where the service resides.

Shadow-page In order to implement recoverable files, the actual file page is not updated. A new block is allocated for the update during which time the page has two versions: the new one and the old or shadow-page.

Shannon's equation A fundamental theorem in communications that defines the channel capacity.

Shift register A register through which the bits are shifted.

SIMD (Single instruction multiple data-stream). A computer which has many processing elements which can perform the same operation on different data items simultaneously.

Simplex A mode of transmission that permits information flow in only one direction.

Single-shot protocol Requests are repeatable and no acknowledgments are returned.

Sinusoidal wave A simple wave with the shape of a sine curve.

Skew The inability to maintain parallel flow in parallel transmissions. Some bits arrive before others.

Slotted aloha A channel access mechanism in which stations transmit packets at the beginning of time slots.

SNA (System Network Architecture) An IBM network architecture.

Station A device that allows user access to the network.

STDM (Statistical time division multiplexing) A technique used to multiplex a channel among several stations. Time slots are allocated based on the expected user demand which allows more user stations than time slots.

Store-and-forward Messages are routed through the network one IMP-to-IMP

IDPC   N

link at a time. A complete end-to-end path is not allocated.

Switch   A device that connects communication channels in order to extend the range of communications.

Synchronization   The programming of different activities so that they operate in step with each other.

Systolic array   An array of processing elements synchronized to execute some algorithm as the data operands flow through the array.

TDM (Time division multiplexing)   The sharing of a single channel among several stations by allocating each station a time slot.

Three-message protocol   A communication protocol that involves a request, response and acknowledgment sequence.

Tightly coupled system   A computer system which contains more than one processor sharing a common memory and controlled by a single operating system.

Time-sharing   The facility to accommodate several users on a single computer at the same time by allocating small time slices to each user.

Timestamp   A time of day tag on a transaction to identify it. This timestamp is usually concatenated with a host number to achieve uniqueness.

Token   A bit frame that indicates an access privilege.

Token access   An access method that is based on the availability of a token.

Token passing   A reference to the passing on of a token among the stations. It is usually seen in ring LANs where the token circulates around the ring.

Topology   This is a reference to shape, which in our case is the shape of a network.

Transmission rate   The rate at which the digits are transmitted.

Transparency   The details of the system are hidden from the user.

Tree model   A software system that is structured like a tree – child nodes have only one parent node.

Tuple   The reference to the row of a relation in the relational database model.

Tuple calculus   A relational calculus that uses tuple variables in forming queries.

Tuple variable   A variable that can have the value of a tuple from a specified relation.

Two-phase commit   A technique used in distributed systems to implement recoverable updates. All participating sites must be coordinated to ensure that all sites behave in the same manner. This involves two phases.

Two-phase lock   A locking protocol used in distributed systems which involves a locking of all needed resources before beginning a transaction, and a release phase. Once a resource is released it cannot be reclaimed.

Undo/redo log   A log file that supports recoverable files. (*See* log file.)

Variable free language   A functional language that does not see variables as representatives of memory locations but as objects to which functions are to be applied.

Vector processor   A processor that can execute the same instruction on a vector of elements in a pipeline manner.

Vertical partitioning   The division of a relation into partitions such that a partition contains some of the attributes for all the tuples.

Virtual call/circuit The same communication path is used for the delivery of all the packets in a message and the sequence is maintained.

Virtual memory A system which allows executable programs to be larger than the primary storage. Programs are divided into pages and held on secondary storage. Pages are mapped onto primary storage blocks at run time.

Virtual terminal A mechanism by which a data structure is used to accommodate terminals of different type.

VLSI Very large scale integrated circuitry.

WAN (Wide area network) *See* long-haul network.

Window size The number of messages that can be sent before receiving acknowledgments in the Go-Back-N protocol.

X-21, X-25 CCITT network access protocols that are incorporated in the ISO-OSI reference model at layers 1, 2 and 3.

INDEX